SELF-PUBLISHING
FOR PASSIVE INCOME

How to Publish a Book on Amazon

Find the Book in You

Everyone has a story to share. Who hasn't thought at one time that they could write a book?

How does an extra $1,000 a month sound? How about $2,000 or more and with no extra work?

Whether you want to share your story, make extra cash every month or both, self-publishing is the way to do it. I've published 10 books and average $200 a month from each. That's $2,000 a month and all I do is spend under $200 on marketing.

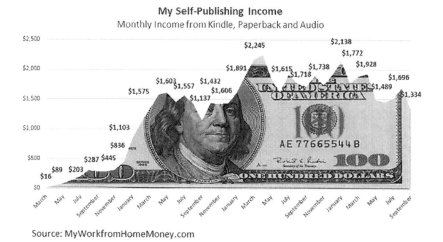

Source: MyWorkfromHomeMoney.com

Against all the ways to make money I've tried, from blogging to Amazon and freelancing, self-publishing is by far the most passive. After you launch your book, there's almost nothing you need to do to collect a stable and consistent income every month.

On ten books, I know I'll always have money in checking at the end of the month to pay the bills. The money from my book sales hit in the last few days of the month and it's always there.

Now that's financial freedom.

Then why isn't everyone publishing books? Why are so many people struggling every day in a job they hate when they could be creating passive income? What have I discovered that only a few know?

As easy as it sounds to self-publish a book, there is a process to do it right and it's not an easy process to start. Of the more than two million books available on Amazon right now, about half make less than $30 a month and many make no sales. To be truly successful, you need to understand the entire process from picking a topic with built-in demand, writing a quality book and getting it in front of the right people.

That's what I'm here to teach you.

I'm going to show you the exact process I use to self-publish a book, from putting your idea together to making it a source for passive income. With what you learn in this book, you won't spend years trying to find someone to publish your book and won't begin one of the thousands of books started each year that never get completed.

With this book, you're just three months from your first self-published book!

What you'll learn in this book:

- How to find and develop a book idea that will be instantly popular with readers. (pg 8)
- The process I use to make writing easy and will make you look like a professional author. (pg 18)

- How I created a $10,000 book description on Amazon that readers can't resist! (pg 72)
- My blueprint for a best-selling book launch! (pg 93)
- Three book marketing strategies that make your book passive income! (pg 103)

Joseph Hogue, CFA

Born and raised in Iowa, Joseph Hogue graduated from Iowa State University after serving in the Marine Corps. He worked in corporate finance and real estate before starting a career in investment analysis. He has appeared on Bloomberg and CNBC and led a team of equity analysts for a venture capital research firm. He holds a master's degree in business and the Chartered Financial Analyst (CFA) designation.

He left the corporate world in 2014 to build his online businesses, first through creating websites and later through YouTube. Booking just $792.41 in 2015 income, he's grown his online assets to an income of $122,400 for the twelve-months to July 2019. He's published 12 books and has grown the YouTube channel, Let's Talk Money, to over 100,000 subscribers in just 18 months.

ISBN

978-1-7331085-3-9 eBook

978-1-706195-3-20   paperback

Contents

Get My Nine Quick-Start Tips NOW!

You'll find everything you need to write, publish and make money on your self-publishing dreams in this book but I wanted to give you a quick-win to get started.

I've seen so many would-be authors get frustrated at the process for writing their book and give up before they have a chance to be successful.

And you CAN be successful as a self-published author. I know you can and I know it's going to be easier than you expect if you really give it a chance.

To show you how easy it can be and to give you that quick shot of motivation to self-publish your book, I put together this free handout, **9 Tips Anyone Can Use to Write a Book**.

It's going to give you the quick-start details to writing your book, getting those first words on the page, so you get the motivation to keep going!

Click here for this free download and get started fast!

Or go to **https://myworkfromhomemoney.com/get-started-publishing**

Finding Your Money-Making Book Idea

Use this self-publishing process to make your book idea a reality in less than six months

How does an extra $1,000 a month sound? How about an extra $2,000 a month or more?

Self-publishing is one of the most passive forms of income I know and so easy to set up. I average an income of $200 a month on the books I've written and can publish a new book in as little as two months.

That means five or six books a year and a consistent income stream every single month.

The potential in self-publishing contrasts with the fact that just one-in-five bloggers use the income stream. Everyone has a book idea in them but not everyone is able to get that idea out and reach their goal of publication.

Finding the perfect book idea and taking it from idea to published book means a months-long process and beating the self-defeating voices that snag even the most experienced authors.

I'm going to share with you the process I've used to self-publish ten books, a process that you can use to have your book making money within a few months.

Setting Your Book Up for Success

Before we get into planning and organizing your first book, there are three tools that will help set you up for success.

First, you need to set a strict schedule and plan for your book. More than researching your topic or learning how to market a self-published book, setting a schedule is one of the most critical steps you'll need to take.

Without a schedule, it's too easy to let life distract you from writing. You'll put off writing the difficult chapters and won't be able to get back into it when you do have time. Months will go buy and the whole project will just become a forgotten folder in your computer.

We'll cover how long each step in the self-publishing process usually takes and how to build a schedule that works for you.

You also need to learn the process of self-publishing from idea through writing and launching your book. Self-publishing isn't just creating a compelling story or writing out how to do something. It's a business and to be successful, you need to learn how that business works.

Without understanding the process of self-publishing, it's just too easy to get lost in all the parts. Learn the process and how to work everything in order in your schedule and you'll be one step closer to a best-seller.

Finally, a positive mindset is a must when starting any kind of a project like this. I know, that sounds like generic advice but developing the right attitude will help you beat all the self-defeating voices in your head.

Every that's ever created something special has had to deal with those voices at some point. You'll get to a point in the book and think, "Who am I to be writing this? It's not like I'm the most successful person in the field," or those voices will question whether anyone will read the book and whether all the work will be worth it.

No one that lets those voices change their path has ever been successful. That doesn't mean you won't fail. It just means that you have to take a risk, you have to put yourself out there to succeed.

Of the ten books I've self-published to this point, four average less than $100 a month in income. What sucks even more is that I thought a two of them were my best books, well-written and with information readers couldn't get anywhere else. But they just haven't done much.

If I worried about rejection or failure every time I set out on a project, I wouldn't average $2,000 a month self-publishing. I wouldn't have five websites that get over 50,000 visitors a month and I'd be stuck in a 9-to-5 with someone always telling me what to do.

Plan out your book. Take the time to learn the material and give your readers something special and you will be successful. You'll reach hundreds of people a month with your book and can cultivate that relationship into a six-figure business.

How to Find the Self-Publishing Writer in You

One of the first questions you might be asking is, what should you write about?

Any business idea or project always needs to come from two places to be successful, something in which you have experience and something you are passionate about. If you can make a business out of those two things, you're almost guaranteed to be successful.

- What are your credentials in and in which fields have you worked?
- What are your hobbies? When you talk with your friends, what topics often come up?

If you don't think there's a book anywhere in the answers to those questions, you obviously haven't been on Amazon lately. Do an Amazon book search for any of your answers to the questions above and you'll find lots of books already published.

Writing a book isn't just about the 'what' of your book's topic but it's just as much why are you writing it.

You're not writing your book to educate readers. You're not writing it to give them information about the topic.

People don't buy books for the information, they buy books for the transformation.

That's why you're writing the book, to transform your readers.

Once you know the general topic on which you want to write, it's the transformation that needs to guide your book.

- What do you want readers to be able to do after reading the book?
- How will readers' lives be different after reading your book?

Answering these two questions will not only help you in planning out your chapters but will help separate your book from the millions on Amazon. Developing your book around that transformation will give it special purpose and serve your readers.

That transformation, thinking about it and using it throughout the entire self-publishing process, is extremely important and we'll come back to it often.

By now, you should have a few ideas for your book. In fact, you might have ideas for several different books.

There's one last trick you can use to develop your book idea and make it excellent.

1. Go to Amazon and do a book search for your topic or idea.
2. Click through each book that seems closely related to your idea
3. In a spreadsheet, note the chapter titles and the transformation the author seems to be getting to in the description.
4. Read through the reviews for each book, both good reviews and bad. What did readers appreciate seeing? Did they have unanswered questions or wish something else was added?

This kind of research is a gold mine for your book. What are other authors talking about and is there anything readers are expecting but not getting? Are most of the books targeted to a specific reader group? Can you target a different, underserved demographic?

After all your research is done, you'll be ready to start planning your book.

The Importance of Planning in Self-Publishing

A lot of new authors just jump right in with a blank word processing document and an idea for their book.

That book never gets finished.

A detailed plan and schedule for your book not only helps keep you on pace but makes writing your book a hundred times easier. Without a good plan, you'll get writer's block and will worry excessively about the different pieces in the self-publishing puzzle.

Take the time to write out a plan for your book! Take your time, at least a couple of days to research ideas and plan everything out.

We'll first cover the process of planning out the book itself and then how to plan the overall self-publishing process.

Planning Your First Book

Planning the book itself starts with outlining the book chapters. Through your brainstorming about book ideas and research in other books in the topic, you should have a pretty good list of large topics that need to be included.

My suggestion is to step back a little and go back to your transformation.

Think about the transformation you want to cause in your readers and work backwards from there. From the transformation, what does the reader need to know to get there?

This will give you a good list of topic ideas for chapters. You can then go back and fill it in with other chapter ideas you got from the research process.

Most books have anywhere from seven to 15 chapters but aim for 10 to 12 chapters. You might have more than ten or twelve chapter ideas but can you fit some of these ideas together in one chapter?

- List out all your chapter ideas and the broad topics that a reader needs to get to the transformation.
- Group the ideas into related topics and themes.
- Combine ideas and themes into chapters until you have ten or twelve distinct steps.

Your book outline isn't done yet. That's just the big picture of how you'll get your readers from introduction to transformation.

You now need to outline each individual chapter. It might seem unnecessarily detailed and remind you of those hated outlining exercises in school but outlining each chapter will make your book easier to write and much easier to read.

The plan for each chapter of your book should be outlined with:

- At least three or four steps or ideas important to the chapter.
- Why the chapter topic is important to the overall transformation and the rest of the book.
- A real-world example or story about the chapter idea or process.

Breaking each chapter down like this into steps and examples will make writing so much easier. It's not so easy to just sit down and start writing on a blank screen. Outlining your chapter puts it into manageable chunks that are easier to handle. You'll be able to sit down and start writing and it will all fit together better once you're done.

I know some authors that outline each chapter as they come to it. I would recommend outlining everything first though. This will help you decide better where different ideas belong in the book and how everything flows from one chapter to the next.

Planning the Self-Publishing Process

The self-publishing process can seem like Dante's Inferno, in other words, "abandon all hope ye who enter here."

It's easy to get discouraged at some point from writing to editing, formatting and launching your book. If there are over four million books available on Amazon, I'd bet there are two or three times that many that were started and never finished.

The process doesn't have to be that long or intimidating though. I'll outline a six-month timeline here, but I know authors that put out a new book each month. I can usually work through the process in two or three months if I don't have too many other projects running at the same time.

Six months to write, develop and launch a book is a good goal if you are working a full-time job and have other responsibilities.

Writing your book will depend on your level of experience and how quickly you write. Try estimating a schedule but then come back to it to revise the timeline after a chapter or two when you have a better idea of how long it's taking.

I like to write at least one chapter a week, so I can publish it to my blog and use that as marketing after the book is launched. If you can't do a chapter a week, try aiming for one every two weeks. That will mean roughly three months of writing for most books.

Editing your book is actually a multi-staged process and will usually take a couple of months if you have people that are willing to edit your book without putting it at the bottom of their to-do list.

- After the book draft is finished, you'll need a developmental edit which makes sure the book flows well from start to finish. This will take at least two weeks and you'll spend another two to four weeks rewriting afterwards to fill in the gaps.
- After the book has been revised, you'll need a copy edit which corrects spelling and grammar mistakes. This will take at least two weeks.

Formatting your book can be done in less than a week depending on whether you do it yourself or hire out the process. It's fairly simple to format your book for Kindle and paperback and you can usually do it in a day yourself.

If you have someone else format your book, make sure you check each final copy for formatting errors like removed spaces and pages with less than a few lines of text.

Creating a cover for your book can take several weeks but is hugely important so don't skimp on this one. If you're not graphically-talented then I'd recommend getting help from a professional.

Have your designer mock-up three or four cover ideas. These don't have to be finished covers but just rough ideas and structure. Put those cover ideas in a side-by-side comparison on Facebook and ask your friends to choose which they like best. Once your network has picked a winner, you designer can finish it out.

It will take around a month to develop your cover like this but you can do it while you're writing so it won't mean additional time on your timeline.

Putting together your Amazon book page is more important than most authors understand and can take a week to do it well. Write out your book description and let it set for a day before coming back to revise. You'll also need to research keywords and categories for your book.

Launching your book is a two-step process between pre-launch and the actual launch itself. Spend at least four weeks pre-launching your book, reaching out to people for launch-week purchases and reviews, and planning other marketing. Your launch will stretch over two weeks of getting those reviews and strategically pricing your book.

Your book doesn't need to be a three-volume series and thousands of pages. Think of your book as a shortcut to the transformation and try getting your reader there as quickly as possible. This usually means at least 120 pages but no more than 220 pages in a 9x6 format. The entire process can be accomplished in less than six months and you'll have an asset that is almost completely passive.

Putting together your book idea is the first critical step in making your book a success. Spending the time to plan out and detail as much as possible will help make everything go much smoother later on. The key to avoiding writer's block and a hundred other self-publishing hurdles is found right here in this first step.

How to Research for Self-Publishing a Book

Researching before writing your book will make self-publishing easy

The number one cause of writer's block is trying to sit down to write a whole book without breaking it down into pieces. The second cause of writer's block, and really related to the first cause, is not researching before you begin writing.

Researching your book will not only help you know what to write but will make it a more thorough book. You'll be able to tell your readers exactly what they need to get to their transformation from start to finish.

There is one caveat to researching your book and this is something we'll talk about more in-depth. There's a fine-line between thoroughly researching what needs to be in your book and getting analysis paralysis. We'll first look at how to research your book and how you can avoid overdoing it to get started fast.

How to Use Amazon to Research Your Book

We'll talk about four resources to research your book but the best is easily going to be Amazon. After all, if you're going to be writing a book for Amazon, why not go right to the source to see what Amazon users want?

Using Amazon to research your book is as easy as browsing other books in the topic. Click through to a few books, I like to focus on those with at least 100 reviews. You'll want to check out other parts of each book's page like the description when you go to publish but here you're going to be looking in the book itself.

Most books will have a 'Look Inside' feature allowing you to preview a portion of the book. Go straight to the table of contents to see how the author is guiding readers from start to transformation.

First, let me answer one question I always get when talking about researching books on Amazon. No, we're not talking about stealing from other authors. While you might buy a few books to brush up on the topic, you're going to be writing from your perspective. Never copy sections or materials from another book.

Another powerful resource for researching your book will come from the Reviews section on each book page. You don't have to read every review. Many of the five-star reviews are from friends and family so not critical enough to give you any good information.

Go to the four-star and the one- or two-star reviews. The four-star reviews will tell you what readers enjoyed, what they were glad was included in the book. The bad reviews will tell you what should have been included, how to make your book a crowd-pleaser.

How to Use Udemy to Research Your Book

Udemy is a video course platform featuring just about every topic imaginable. Don't believe me? Just browse some of the video courses and you'll find things like, "How to Solve a Rubik's Cube," and "How to Parallel Parking."

This makes it an excellent resource for researching because you're sure to find several courses on your book's topic. Since these are explicitly 'courses' they go directly to the point of teaching students how to get to a transformation. That means they're usually laid out in a less roundabout way compared to some of the books you'll find on Amazon.

Clicking through to each course, you'll find several points for research. First, you'll see some marketing content that can guide you in writing up your own marketing material and book page on Amazon. Further down the page, you'll find a Table of Contents to everything in the course.

Another benefit to using Udemy as a research resource is that course outlines are generally more descriptive than book chapters on Amazon. You'll find on Amazon that many authors will try to be 'cute' with naming their chapters. Instead of describing the chapter, the title will be a play on words or some other nonsense.

On Udemy, the course contents are always descriptive of what you'll learn in each section. Creators want to tell potential students exactly what they'll learn in each module. Some courses even have a preview video where you'll find a summary of everything covered.

How to Use Google to Research Your Book

Google is the first place I go to research new posts for my blogs. It's a quick resource for smaller articles but also a great place to find ideas for your book.

You'll want to take this one chapter-by-chapter, researching each step in your transformation. That means taking each chapter idea and searching for it on Google.

The first thing you'll notice, typing anything into the search bar on Google, is that it will start suggesting ideas. Pay attention to what is suggested. These are the most popular searches that start with your keywords and can be ideas on what people are looking for when they think in your topic terms.

A new addition to the search results on Google is the 'People Also Ask' section, displaying four or five questions related to the topic. Clicking on any of these will populate a new question or two at the bottom of the list. Not all of these will be directly related or relevant to your book idea but it's a solid resource to use.

After checking out these questions, scroll down to the end of the search results for the 'People Also Search' section. These aren't as useful as the related questions but can still give you ideas on what should be included in each chapter.

Clicking through a few of the top search results will show you what bloggers are saying about the topic. Google has already done the work for you by sorting the results by quality so these top results should be detailed and include a lot of good ideas for your chapter.

This process of looking through the top Google search results is actually a great blogging strategy as well. Doing this for each post you write helps to ensure a detailed and informative article that includes points Google already sees as authoritative. It's a great way to rank your posts, triggering the Google algorithm by hitting the important points.

Finally, you'll want to find a few blogs that are narrowly focused on your book topic. Most will include a 'Best of' section on the side of the blog, highlighting the most popular articles. This can be another good resource for finding chapter ideas.

How to Use YouTube to Research Your Book

Let's look at one more resource tool before talking about why you don't necessarily need to use all the resources listed. There's a point where you can have too much research but don't overlook YouTube as one potential.

YouTube is a little like Udemy in your book research. You'll find informative videos on just about any topic. They might not be as direct or detailed as the ones uploaded to Udemy but the upside to YouTube is that you'll be able to watch the video for free.

After watching a few videos on your topic, YouTube will start to suggest other related videos in your home feed and on the right-side of the page. These can offer more ideas for topics. You'll also want to click through to channels narrowly-focused on the topic, then click on Videos in the menu. By sorting by popularity, you can get an idea for which sub-topics or ideas are more popular among viewers.

Putting All Your Research Together

Now that I've shown you all these resources for researching your book, it's time to come back from the ledge. I don't want to say too much research is just as bad as too little, but there's definitely a risk.

Too many would-be authors get stuck in the research stage. They want everything to be perfect, spending weeks looking for every detail. They end up getting discouraged from the lack of progress and ultimately give up.

It's called analysis paralysis and it's one of the biggest obstacles to your book.

Avoiding analysis paralysis means setting a firm deadline for research. Give yourself a week or two to get the information you need and then get to writing!

It won't take long to put together pages of notes from your research. Doing your research by chapter will help to organize your notes. Even within each chapter though, everything has to fit somewhere.

Don't be afraid to drop random or unnecessary ideas if they don't fit in a section somewhere. You want your book to be detailed but not bogged down in the minutiae. The best books are the ones that take readers from start to transformation in the fewest steps necessary.

This means you might not need every resource listed above. I like using YouTube but only because I'm on the platform so frequently anyway. Watching videos can side-track your process and take up valuable time so this is probably the first resource I'd consider dropping. Start with Udemy and Amazon for your research and then fill in details with the other two platforms.

Researching your book before writing will make the process so much faster. You'll ensure you get all the detail you need in your book to help your readers and you'll make writing easier. Balance this need for research with the need to avoid analysis paralysis and get your book started.

How to Write a Book [the Easy Way]

You don't need to be a writer to write a book, you just need a process

Everyone has a book idea in them. How many times have you thought to yourself, "That would make a great book. I should write that." There's something deep in us all to share our life experiences and what we know.

So why aren't there more books written?

The problem is, somewhere along the way, people got the impression you had to be a 'writer' to write a book. They think you have to be a salty old man with a beard and a glass of scotch to write a book.

If you've ever written an email, a social media update or directions on a post-it note...you're a writer. You've got what it takes to write a book.

Writing a full book is just organizing your idea beyond a few notes. I'll cover a simple process to organizing and writing out your book then some writing exercises to develop your skills.

3 Rules that Will Make Writing Easy

We'll get to the process I've used to write ten self-published books but three rules will keep you on track and guarantee your success.

- Organize your research and content. The more organized you are with outlines for each chapter, the easier it will be to write everything out.
- Stay motivated. Have clearly defined short-term goals like writing a chapter a week to motivate you with

forward progress. Connect with another author or group to support and motivate each other.

- Treat it like a job. Schedule time to write every single day and ignore all distractions while you're writing.

The Writing Process

The misconception about writing is that it comes from inspiration. People think professional writers are somehow magically inspired and just sit down at the computer from which the words flow.

Admittedly, Stephan King and John Grisham aren't in my circle of close friends. Maybe this is how it works for the masterminds of literature...but not for the vast majority of authors. For most authors, it's all about the process.

The writing process is a simple step-by-step to understanding what you want to write about and putting the words on the page as efficiently as possible. It's the process I've used to write ten books and every author I know uses some form of this method.

Understanding Your Purpose

These first two steps of the process will largely be done in your research for the book. Understanding your purpose just means knowing the transformation you want to drive in your readers. What is the ultimate goal of your book, how do you want readers to grow from it.

With the transformation in mind, you can work backwards through each step to reach it.

Understanding Your Reader

Not only do you need to understand the transformation you want readers to achieve, but understand why they want to achieve it. That means understanding your reader, who they are and where they come from.

- At what level of information are your readers coming from? Writing for novices will mean something differently than if you assume your readers already have some level of knowledge in the subject.
- Why do readers want to achieve the transformation? What motivates them, what are the basic needs that drive them? Neglect these questions and your readers will lack the motivation to finish the book.
- What are your readers' major obstacles to starting and achieving the transformation? Where are the biggest roadblocks within the process? Knowing this can help you add more detail where needed to make sure your readers don't get stuck.

Outlining Each Chapter

After all your research and notes around your idea, you're likely to have pages of what will look like a jumbled mess for each chapter. Trying to write from this is just going to be frustrating chaos.

Your next step is to organize all your notes into an outline for each chapter. That starts with writing out the main idea for each chapter, each section heading then the notes that apply to each. For example, here's the start of my outline for this chapter. For brevity, I've removed some of the detail but you can still see how everything is lined up in manageable chunks.

- Why most people fail to write a book, think you need to be an author
- Using a process makes it so anyone can write a book
  - Rules for Writing
    - Organize and research
    - Stay motivated
    - Treat it like a job
  - The process
    - Understanding purpose
    - Understanding reader
    - Outlining
    - Adding stories and anecdotes
  - My book writing strategy
    - Integrating book with a blog
      - Natural fit for bloggers
      - Easy marketing channel
      - Feedback on each chapter
    - Writing each chapter as a post then format into entire book, adding calls-to-action within each post
  - Writing exercises
    - Purpose
    - Readers
    - Finding different perspectives
    - Telling the story

Just as with working backwards from your transformation to each step a reader needs to take, you can use this idea in each chapter as well. What steps do your reader need to take to progress on to the next chapter.

Breaking your book into chapters, then into main points for each chapter and sections, you can see how much easier it is to write it out. You know exactly what you want to say and each section might only be half a page. I like to aim for at least ten pages per chapter, that's about 2,000 words for a standard 6x9 formatted book. That's not a strict rule and just writing out from your outline, you're likely to go well over 10 pages anyway.

Adding Stories, Anecdotes and Examples

Stories and examples are critical to the success of your book. Readers can go anywhere for the information. What makes your book special is the first-hand and personal experience you share. Adding stories and examples to your book will make it more interesting and relatable for readers.

Writing out your book, many of these stories will happen naturally. Humans are natural story-tellers. It's how we've evolved, passing down information through personal experiences and triumphs.

But you should also go back through your book, after your first draft, to find places to include more of these anecdotes. That's how critical they are to your book. Again, there's no rule that you need a story every chapter but I like to try including one. Whether it's to relate important points, inspire or help readers through the most difficult concepts, a good story can bring your book to life.

A Writing Strategy to Sell More Books

I've referred to my self-publishing strategy for bloggers a few times but wanted to detail it in a separate section. This strategy works on so many levels and really makes writing easy. It will not only become your best source for marketing but will keep you on schedule to publish.

- Write out each chapter as a blog post, once a week. This sets a reasonable pace and keeps you on schedule.
- Promote each blog post on social media, through your email list and ask for feedback on how the post can be improved.
- When all your chapters are done, combine them into one document. Remove any references to blog posts

and read through to make sure the story flows naturally from chapter to chapter.

- Revise and add content to each chapter according to feedback and anything you've learned through the process.
- After your book is published, add a paragraph or two into each blog post about the book and include a link to your Amazon page.

Not only will the strategy keep you on schedule but it's a stress-free way to develop each chapter. Nobody expects a blog post to be perfect so you can write out your chapters first and then refine them before publishing. You'll also get some great feedback from readers on each chapter so you make sure you hit every point.

Writing Exercises to Develop Your Skills

I can show you the entire process to researching and putting together a book but a lot of successful writing is about practice and knowing what to practice. I've edited and republished old blog posts and old books several times because I've never stopped practicing to become a better writer.

Not only will the writing exercises here help you develop your skills but they will also help organize and plan your book. Each of these exercises should be at least a page or two so try writing out as much detail as possible.

1) The why of your book. Write out a plan for your book, why do you want to write it and the goals you want to help readers achieve.

- Will your book help readers do something or accomplish something?
- What do readers need to be successful in the subject?

- What do you want to share with your readers, emotionally or analytically?
- Is your book meant to get someone started or to help advanced readers in the subject?

This writing exercise will help you with organization and writing out a process. By the time you're done, you should have a good idea of outline and your book's value to readers.

2) Write out two avatars for your target readers. This means writing out a biography of two types of readers that are most likely to buy your book.

- Where are they at in their lives? Are they young adults looking for direction? Are they older readers looking for something new? Do they just want to escape into another reality for a few hours?
- What demographics define your reader? (location, age, gender, income, educational level, religion, ethnicity, marital status)
- What is your reader thinking? Why do they want to learn about the subject? What are the questions they have about it? How important is it to them, as a hobby or as a job?

There are a few ways to research some of these points.

- Search Reddit within categories around your topic. Reddit is an answer and conversation platform categorized around subjects. It's a great resource for finding the most common questions people have and perspectives in a topic.
- Search for internet forums on the topic. This will also show you common questions and discussion points.
- Do a Google search for questions and keywords around your topic. Besides just reading articles in the results,

Google might also display other questions to consider in the "People also ask," section.

- If you have a blog or know someone with a blog in the topic, you can look at Google Analytics to see demographic data around visitors.

You don't necessarily need data to support all of this. Part of the exercise is thinking creatively to build a reader persona. Write out something like a two-page biography of their life with everything that led them to your book.

This exercise develops empathy for your reader, putting yourself in their shoes and understanding what they need from your book.

3) Devil's advocate. Non-fiction writers need to be able to give their readers every perspective and a fair assessment of the subject. This means being able to think objectively about the topic rather than only relying on your own opinions and perception.

Pick two topics about which you feel strongly, maybe about a political ideology or a social cause. Write out two pages arguing for the other perspective, the side of the argument you wouldn't normally support.

This is probably going to take some research. You could write out your own viewpoint easily but may not know as much about the other side's argument. Don't assume you know the other side, do a Google search and read through a few articles.

Don't just go through the motions on this one. Really try to convince someone in your writing to take the other side of the topic.

You'll want to use this level of objective writing into your book research as well. This exercise will help develop that mentality to give your readers both sides and every perspective on the subject.

4) Learning to teach. Non-fiction writers need to be able to teach, from the simplest of tasks to detailing long and complicated processes.

Pick two tasks, one that is simple and another that would be complicated for most people. Create a step-by-step process for each task, detailing everything a reader new to the subject would need.

If you can, find someone with no knowledge of the tasks to read through your guide. If they can perform the tasks then you did a good job of teaching. Ask them questions about the tasks to make sure they understand completely.

This exercise helps to develop your process writing and teaching skills.

5) Telling the story. Even non-fiction writers need to tell stories. A personal story around the topic will help your readers relate to the material and see how it unfolds in real life.

First, tell your own story. Pick a day or an event in your life and write out your auto-biography.

- How did you feel and how did the day change your life?
- Be dramatic in your story. Describe your emotions and those of the people around you. Use descriptive adjectives to bring the story to life.
- Touch on as many emotions as possible including humor, fear and surprise.

Next, go somewhere public and pick out someone you don't know. Jot down a few things you notice about them; what they're wearing, their way of walking and carrying themselves. Write out a story about them and their day. Remember, you don't really know this person so be creative and just make up a story.

Not only will this exercise help to develop your creativity but it will also help practice making your book relatable through personal stories.

Getting More from Your Book

That gives you a process for writing your book and getting published. I've got a few more ideas on how to get the most from your book, how to make a little more money and create a community.

These ideas all involve adding links and special sections into your book's content. It takes almost no additional effort but can go a long way to getting more from your book.

- Add a page highlighting an additional handout or checklist free for downloading. Link to a landing page where the reader can download the handout by signing up to an email list. One of the biggest shortcomings of Amazon is you have no idea who bought your book. This gives you a list of readers to remarket for other books and products.
- Reference affiliate products with a link throughout the book where appropriate and in a resources page at the end. If someone clicks through and makes a purchase, you get a commission on the sale.
- Add a link to your own products and other books on the resources page.

It doesn't take a special gift to write a book, just a plan and a little practice. You may never be as successful as J.K. Rowling or as well-known as Shakespeare but you can easily make a lot of money self-publishing. Follow this proven process and writing exercises to put your ideas to words. Stay on schedule by blogging your chapters and you'll be on track to publish in less than a few months.

How to Edit a Book for Self-Publishing

Understanding the book editing process and how to find a good editor could make all the difference and lead to self-publishing success.

There are more than four million books available on Amazon and a lot of them are crap. They're poorly written, more like a list of ideas and readers get through less than half the book on average. It's why the majority of self-published books sell less than a few hundred copies, not in a year but over their entire lifetime.

Why? Poor editing.

Anyone can write a book. Even if your grammar is less than perfect or you often misspell words, you still have a great story that needs to be told.

The problem is that it's too easy to self-publish. Anyone can write a book but not everyone takes the time to write a good book.

Editing not only fixes bad spelling and grammar but will help your readers get everything they can out of your book. It will help get your message across and make you look like a professional author.

How do I know? Because I was always an average student in English and writing classes, nothing special. I've self-published ten books. None have an average rating less than 4 ½ out of five stars and have received over 300 reviews.

Believe me, if my books hadn't been meticulously edited, I would have seen it. I've seen other books that were not edited and readers are brutal in their reviews.

So, editing is critical to publishing a successful book…but you can't edit your own books!

We'll cover what editors do, how to find a good editor and some tools you can use in this article but that doesn't mean you should do it yourself.

So I know talking about editing isn't exactly what you love to do during your free time. It's not the fun part of self-publishing but it's so important to making your book successful.

You've taken the time to write a great book, now it's time to get the help that will make your book a best-seller!

Types of Editing You Need for Your Book

We'll get to why you shouldn't edit your own book in a minute but first let's talk about the types of editing a book needs and the process before it can be published.

Editing isn't just looking for grammar mistakes and misspelt words. A book usually goes through at least three types of edits and sometimes several edits for each type.

- Story or developmental editing is the first step after you're done writing. This edit is to make sure the story flows well in a fiction book or that a non-fiction book is laid out in a way that effectively teaches the material.

- Copy editing is what most people think of when they think of editing. This is where an editor will look for grammar mistakes and spelling problems.

- Proof editing is the final stage of editing and is completed after the book has been formatted.

A developmental editor will look at the book first to make sure it makes sense for readers.

In a fictional story, are the characters developed well and does the story unfold well? Is it interesting and has the author left anything out that helps the reader understand characters' motives or actions? Does the story have plot holes or make factual sense?

In a non-fiction book, the developmental editor will make sure the chapters are structured to best teach the material to readers. Are important points left out that readers need or does the book leave questions unanswered? Is the material factually accurate?

Working with a developmental editor usually means at least a round or two of editing and rewriting before you can send the book to the next stage in editing.

A copy editor will check the writing style, grammar, spelling and word usage in a book. No, just using the spellcheck in Microsoft Word isn't enough. A good editor will find awkward sentences, misspelled words that word processing software missed and will help you make your book more easily readable.

After your book has been checked by a copy editor and revised, you are ready to have it formatted for different types of media. This means putting it into a layout that can be viewed as a digital ebook, printed or listened to as an audio book.

After you book has been formatted, a proof reader will take one final look at each format. This usually covers the same points as the copy editor, but the proof reader is just making sure nothing got changed in formatting. The proof reader will check each format of your book individually, so they'll be reading your ebook, paperback and listening to the audio version.

Don't neglect this last proof reading step. You'd be surprised how many spaces get deleted, how many sentences get moved or removed and just how many little problems can come up through formatting.

Why can't you just use the same person for all your editing? Is someone that can tell you if the book reads well and makes sense going to be the same person that can spot all the grammar and spelling problems? Probably not.

Finding different editors for your book will take advantage of each one's specific talent. It will also avoid the burnout that comes when one person tries to read the same book several times for different types of edits.

Why You Shouldn't Edit Your Own Book

You've spent months writing this book. Now you're looking at having to read through it multiple times for editing and proofreading.

It's not going to work. You are just too close to the book to do a good job editing.

In the developmental edit, you'll assume too much. You know the material so well that you won't be able to see what's missing. You'll be reading the book, but your brain will automatically fill in all the missing pieces from your experience.

In copy editing, you'll have a tendency to read too quickly and won't catch the mistakes. You're pretty sure you didn't make many mistakes so probably won't find that many, right?

Nobody speaks in perfectly-placed grammar, but most people think their writing style is good. The problem is that your own writing and word usage is so natural that it feels right even if it sounds awkward to the average reader.

Finally, by the time you get to proof reading, you'll be so tired of reading your book that you'll just skim through and assume everything looks good.

Finding Editors to Review Your Book

There's nothing wrong with asking friends and family to check over your book. If you've got people in your network that do editing for a living or are just really picky when it comes to grammar, even better.

Understand that getting someone to edit your book as a favor might be different from getting someone to do a good job editing your book. We want to do favors for our friends but we're all busy. The temptation will be there for your friends to agree to reviewing your book but then just go through the motions when editing.

The best way to solve this problem is by breaking the book into sections and asking people to review a few chapters. Give someone only as much as they can read in 40 minutes and they're more likely to do a better job editing.

This is harder to do with developmental editing because the person reviewing the book needs to check it from start to finish. My suggestion is to find one or two people that are really excited to support you and use them for your developmental edit. You can then find a few people to check sections of the book for copy editing.

For the developmental edit, make sure you ask your editors questions and talk to them about the book. We'll get into this more in the next section on how to work with editors but having a conversation about the book is a great way to understand if your editor understood the material and got everything out of it.

Even if you have several friends that are willing to help edit your book, it's still a good idea to hire at least one professional. A professional editor is going to know what to look for and common mistakes writers make. They're also going to approach the job as something they want to do well so they can get more of your work in the future.

I've used Upwork for a lot of my book editing and formatting. Upwork is one of the largest freelancer marketplaces, connecting people with tasks to freelancers around the world.

Finding a freelancer on Upwork, or any freelancer marketplace, is easy. Finding a quality freelancer is not always so easy. For editing and other tasks where English proficiency is critical, I would recommend being strict in your requirements for the project. Demand that applicants be fluent or native in English and you might just want to limit your search to countries where English is the native language.

Using Upwork is fairly easy. You start a job, describing what you need and how much you are willing to pay. You can pay by the hour or on a project-basis. I recommend offering a set price for the project.

Once your job is live, freelancers will start to bid on it. Most will place a bid at or close to the price you offered but some will go higher and lower.

Costs for different types of book editing are going to vary depending on a few factors.

- Do you need someone with years of experience or can you get by with a novice editor? Using friends and some basic online editing tools can help take some of the burden so a novice editor will suffice.

- Is your book in a complex subject and targeted to experts? If you need an expert for your developmental edit then you may have to pay more for that expert's time.
- Do you need it done yesterday? You might get an editor to rush your project to the top of their list but it's going to cost you.
- How good a writer are you? The more work an editor has to do, the more they are going to charge you. Again, using online editing tools and a few light edits by friends will help clean up your rough draft.

In general, copy editing will cost from $0.005 to $0.015 per word. Developmental editing and proof reading usually costs a little less, between $0.0025 to $0.0075 per word. These numbers are from the Editorial Freelancers Association. They are a little high by my experience but not by much.

For a standard 35,000-word book (around 170 pages), that means $175 for developmental editing and $350 for copy editing. For an experienced editor from an English-speaking country, I would try offering $150 for your developmental edit and $250 for the copy editing. If you don't get any qualified applicants, you can always increase the offer.

Another great resource for finding editors is college job boards and Craigslist pages for cities with a university. Offering a college student $200 for copy editing is like giving them a year's worth of Ramen noodles! Look for students with a major in your book's topic and offer $100 for developmental edits or students with an English or writing major and offer $200 for copy editing

How to Work with Book Editors

Make sure to ask your editor to turn on 'Track Changes' in their word processing software. This is under the Review tab in Microsoft Word and will note any changes they make when editing the draft. They'll be able to add comments or questions in the margin. You'll also be able to approve any changes they make or delete their change and return to your original draft.

Make sure you check your editors' work. Nobody is perfect, especially if you're hiring less experienced freelance editors. Besides catching your editors' mistakes, you might also want to ignore some of their changes and use your original copy.

Professional developmental editors will have suggestions for your draft but you'll want to have a list of questions you ask to see exactly what they got out of the material. Ask them to describe sections or concepts in their own words. For fictional stories, ask them why they think the characters made certain decisions. You're basically becoming an English teacher here, testing your editors to make sure they understood the material.

Make sure to run your book through a spelling and grammar check one last time to catch anything that might have been changed or missed.

After everything is done, put the book down for a week. Then come back and do one last read through.

Using Editing Tools to Check Your Book

There are several tools online that will help you edit your book. I would recommend using at least one of these, especially if you have friends and family do your editing, but even if you hire a professional editor. The tools are inexpensive and can help catch those last few mistakes that would have ruined a reader's experience.

AutoCrit is specifically for fiction writers. The program checks dialogue, word choice, repetition and will help steer you away from passive voice and clichés. You choose the genre of book and upload your draft for nearly-instant feedback. The $29.97 monthly membership gives you unlimited access to the software.

Hemingway App works a lot like AutoCrit but works for non-fiction as well and includes some great additional features. The app gives you a 'Readability Grade' that breaks down estimated read time, paragraph length and writing style. After uploading your draft, the app uses color highlighting to easily show mistakes and suggestions.

You download the Hemingway App so it's just a one-time cost versus a monthly fee like other tools. You can use it off-line and the app lets you publish directly to Wordpress, Medium, Microsoft Word or to HTML.

Grammarly is the most popular grammar checker but will also spot word usage problems and awkward sentences. The program includes a plagiarism checker that will search for duplicate content on the internet, a good tool if you have some of your book written by freelancers. Grammarly costs $29.95 per month but you can get a discounted price for paying quarterly or annually.

Thorough editing will mean the difference between self-publishing success and a book that gets slammed by readers. It's one of the easiest steps in self-publishing but also one that gets neglected by too many new writers. Unless your Uncle is an English teacher, it's going to cost a little to get professional editors but it is money well spent.

Double Your Book Sales with a Great Cover

Learn what makes a great book cover idea to set your book apart and make more sales

One of the worst elements in self-publishing is the cover. I say worst because the cover is so important to your book but has almost no relevance to the quality within.

You can write one the most spectacular books ever written and get rave reviews but will still make almost no sales if the cover isn't interesting and persuasive.

The fact is that people are scanning through dozens of books on Amazon. Scrolling through as fast as their mouse will go and are only looking at two things, the title and the cover.

My first book, released early in 2015, had miserable sales over the first three months. I was averaging less than $100 a month and working hard to promote it. I redesigned the cover, relaunched the book and saw sales almost triple immediately.

Almost three years later and the book still averages nearly $300 a month in sales and with almost no promotion on my part.

I recommend outsourcing your book cover if graphic design isn't something you enjoy AND are really good at doing. I'll guide you through creating a great cover idea for your book and the strategy I use to make sure my covers are fan favorites.

Finding Your Book Cover Idea

The first step in creating a great book cover is finding your concept, the message you want to send with your cover.

- What's your book's purpose? What transformation are you trying to achieve?
- What emotions do you want to evoke with your cover? Even non-fiction books can evoke emotions.
- What's your book's genre?

For fiction novels, emotion plays a huge role and you want to tap into the theme of your story. For non-fiction books, can you tap into emotions like achievement or inspiration?

Remember, people don't buy the information, they buy the transformation so tap into that with your book cover.

Put the answers to these questions into a list for your concept idea. This list will help you choose images, fonts and cover designs later.

I'll show you how to get ideas from Amazon later but you'll want to do a search through the genre or categories related to your book when trying to create a concept.

Tips for a Great Book Cover Design

I don't know how they teach graphic design in school. My last art class was in 9th grade and I didn't really like it that much. I know what I like in art and I know what book covers do well from almost three years of self-publishing.

You don't have to be an artist to create a book cover design that will attract readers.

So what makes for a great book cover?

1) Minimalism is popular and for good reason. This is the idea that 'less is more', that your cover shouldn't include too many graphics or too much text.

Two seems to be a magic number for book covers. Two colors and two fonts evoke just enough contrast but are not too confusing or too busy.

Minimalism also works for one very important reason. Potential readers aren't going to see the 6x9 version of your cover, they are likely going to see a 67x100 thumbnail first when they browse through books. That's about one inch by 1.5 inches and your cover needs to look good at that size.

2) Don't be afraid to create your own images.

Stock images from sites like Depositphotos and Shutterstock can work but they are usually too generic and don't evoke the kind of emotions or creativity you want.

One important idea for non-fiction authors is branding. If you are planning on working in a niche and want to build a brand around your work, consider using your own image somewhere on the cover. This kind of brand-building can lead to other income sources like sponsorships and speaking engagements.

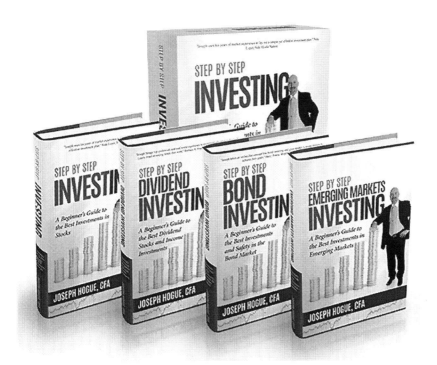

Images need to be the right size for ebook format. The 6x9 cover format is the most widely used and means your cover will be around 1800x2700 pixels. This is a cover ratio of 1.5 to 1 but I've seen 1.6:1 used as well.

3) Don't overlook the power of good fonts.

Fonts are the style of your text and can mean a big difference in your book cover. Using the generic fonts that come with Microsoft Word can make your book look ordinary.

Using two fonts seems to work best, one flashy font for the title and a simpler font for the author name and other text. Good choices for fonts include:

- Bebas neue
- Optimus princeps
- Trajan pro

- Garamond pandama
- Lato
- Open sans or Liberation sans

Don't use more than one 'flashy' font because it will confuse your reader and make the cover look disorganized.

4) Choosing your cover color scheme

Two is the standard for number of colors but three will work as well. Most covers use complimentary colors, two colors opposite each other on the color wheel, for the right amount of contrast.

Orange and teal are popular as well as some of the blues. Whatever you do, avoid the red/green combination unless it's a Christmas thriller.

Stealing a Perfect Book Cover Idea

Since I've never considered myself artistically-gifted, I've always deferred to other book covers for my ideas. This means going to Amazon and Pinterest to find great book cover ideas you can use in your own design.

In Pinterest, you can search for the topic and niche ideas related to your book. Look for what font and color combinations work best together and what emotions come up often in the images.

In Amazon, you can browse the categories most closely related to your book or the genre for fiction novels.

I like to create what's called a 'swipe' file of all the best covers and then use it to brainstorm my own cover.

1. Create a file folder called 'book cover swipe file'

2. Whenever you see a particularly interesting cover on Amazon or Pinterest, right-click and save the image in your swipe file

Putting all the really attractive covers together in a file like this, instead of spread among other covers on Amazon, helps to more easily see commonalities. You'll be able to step back a little, let your eyes see many covers at once, and pick out common ideas used in the group.

Tools to Create Your Own Book Cover

I've always outsourced the actual cover creation of my books after that first disastrous attempt to do my own. It's not as expensive as you might imagine, and you'll make up for the costs many times over with higher sales.

There are tools available if you want to do the actual creation of your book cover. Everyone should have a part in generating the concepts and elements, i.e. images, fonts and colors, but not everyone will actually want to put it all together.

Canva is a free graphic design tool online you can use to make covers for a lot of different formats. I use the tool for the social media feature images for my blog posts. The free service is all most will need but you can get custom designs and graphics for a good price as well.

Adobe is the standard for many designers although there is a learning curve to get familiar with the software.

I've seen authors do their cover with Microsoft Word and other basic word processing software but it never comes out as professional-looking as it could with design software. Why use a steak knife when what you really need is a scalpel?

Whether you are creating the cover yourself or outsourcing it, the design must look good as a thumbnail. After you've got a mock-up of the idea, reduce the size to about 67x100 pixels and make sure you can read the title and that the cover still sends your message.

My Book Cover Strategy for Outsourcing

You don't have to spend hundreds on a great book cover. In fact, I usually spend less than $100 to get multiple ideas and formats.

Start on Fiverr and hire several designers to create mock-up covers based on your cover ideas. Each mock-up will only cost $5 so you can get four or five created. There are other design sites like 99Designs but it usually means hiring designers for at least $25 for each test idea.

Pick three or four of these cover mock-ups and combine them in one side-by-side image. Upload this to Facebook and ask your friends to vote on which they like best. Ask them why they liked each and what they didn't like about the others.

This is a great test for finding the fan favorite cover. I've used the test for five of my books and the winner in four of the tests ended up being the one I probably wouldn't have picked on my own.

Not only will you get some great feedback for your cover but your network will feel like they have some buy-in in the process. That's going to translate to more help when you go to launch your book.

Once you've picked which cover design you want to use, even if it takes a couple of tests, you can hire one designer to finish it. This is where you might consider using someone on 99Designs or paying a little extra to your favorite designer from Fiverr.

You'll need several different formats and sizes of your cover to use in different promotions and places.

- Amazon Kindle requires your cover be at least 1000 pixels wide but optimum is around 2500 pixels wide
- Audible book covers must be no smaller than 2400x2400
- You'll want a flat image and a 3D image of your cover
- Get multiple image sizes of your 3D format, i.e. a thumbnail and a few larger sizes
- Get a multi-media image of the book including a 3D cover next to a box-set or a bundle of your series.
- Get a 728x90 and 300x250 banner of the book and some ad copy to use in your sidebar

You'll also want to make sure you get the source files for your book cover from the designer. This will make it easier to make changes or get new formats made in the future.

Creating a great book cover doesn't have to mean hours spent learning graphic design or that you need to be an artist. Anyone can put together their own cover ideas and then get professional help creating their cover, even on a budget. Spending a little extra time and money on your book cover will pay off with consistent sales every month and will make you look like a professional author.

How to Format a Book for Self-Publishing

Formatting a book for self-publishing is surprisingly easy and can be done in a few simple steps

Formatting a book for self-publishing is one of the least popular topics in publishing but one where I get the most questions. The myth is that formatting for Kindle or other channels is too technical and something most people would be better off outsourcing.

I believed that myth for a long time, paying a freelancer to format my books before publishing.

The truth is that doing your own formatting is a matter of a few clicks and something anyone can do. It will take you less than an hour and maybe half that when you get comfortable with the process.

I'm sharing my entire process for book formatting including how to format the Kindle, paperback and digital copies of your book.

What is Book Formatting and Why is it so Important

Book formatting is the instructions on how your text is laid out. It's the invisible queues that you usually don't even think about when reading like how new chapters start on a new page and the spacing between lines.

Formatting your book is hugely important though because it affects your reader's experience. A book with text that runs together or where the font-type changes will be difficult to read. Besides grammar and spelling, poor formatting is one of the biggest reasons readers leave bad reviews and too many bad reviews will kill your book sales.

Having a process for formatting your book is important because each medium you use to sell your book, i.e. Kindle, paperback and digital may have different requirements for formatting. The formatting that looks good on Kindle isn't necessarily the best and easiest to read when your book is printed.

Book formatting isn't as difficult as you might imagine though and you can do it yourself in less than an hour.

What Types of Documents Do You Need to Sell Your Book?

I write all my books up in Microsoft Word. The word processing software makes it easy to format and save for different channels including Kindle and paperback.

You can also convert your book into other formats like epub, mobi and pdf. You may need epub to upload your print book to platforms like Nook or Lulu but Word will work for most platforms. You'll also want to convert your book into an audio version to sell on Audible but we already covered that in a prior article.

A quick note here about getting an ISBN, short for International Standard Book Number. This is the 10- or 13-digit number that identifies all books published since 1970. You will need a different ISBN for each format of your book including digital, paperback and audio. Amazon will assign a free ISBN for your Kindle version but you may need to buy one for other versions.

The website Bowker.com is the official ISBN agency in the United States and Australia and sells the numbers through its website.

How to Format Your Book for Amazon Kindle

Formatting your book for publication on Amazon Kindle will take less than an hour and maybe half that time once you get comfortable with the process.

First, you'll need to prepare the first pages of your book. These are everything from after the cover but before the first chapter. Most books include a title page, copyright page and table of contents but you can also include a dedication page and a preface.

The first page in your book file should be your title page. Don't confuse this with your book cover. The title page is a separate page that shows your title and sub-title. You will upload the book cover separately from the book file.

- Your title page should include the title, sub-title and the author name
- Center the text by clicking on the Home tab in the menu and then the Center button in the paragraph tab
- Insert a page break after the last text on the page. Click Insert in the menu and then Page Break in the left-most tab

The copyright page usually follows and has the same formatting but where the title is usually centered at the middle of the title page, copyright information is usually centered at the bottom of the page.

Copyright (c) 2018 [Your Company]

All Rights Reserved

If you want to dedicate the book to someone, that will usually follow the copyright page. Center the text and insert a page break afterwards.

To my wife and kids for all their support.

The table of contents not only acts as a guide for your readers but will also be used in Kindle to navigate through the book. Page numbers don't appear in Kindle, but readers can click on each chapter in the table to go directly to that spot in the book.

Each chapter title throughout your book should be formatted in a 'heading' style of your font. This is easily done by selecting each chapter title (throughout the book, not in the table of contents). Then click on Home in the menu and click on Heading 1 in the 'Styles' tab.

Once all your chapter titles are marked as Headings, you can put your table of contents in the front part of your book.

- On your Table of Contents page click on References in the Word menu and then click 'Table of Contents' in the left-most tab. A drop-down will show with a few different choices for formatting.
- Choose one of the first two ToC formats and a box will appear. Uncheck the box for 'Show Page Numbers' and set the 'Show levels' box to 1
- Click OK and your table of contents will show on the page

Setting a bookmark on your table of contents page tells Kindle where to find it.

- Highlight the "Table of Contents" text on your page and click Insert in the menu
- Click on Bookmark in the Links tab and type "toc" (without quotes) and click add

This will create a professional-quality Table of Contents your readers can use in Kindle to navigate through the book.

Your Preface or Prologue sections, both optional, will be formatted like any other chapter in the book and be followed by a page break.

Formatting the rest of your book for Kindle is even easier with just a few steps you need to take for the general text. We'll cover this in the 'More Formatting Tips' below.

Convert your ma_nuscript to HTML format

- Save the file as a "Filtered HTML document" by clicking File then Save As in the menu. Then select Web Page Filtered (*htm, *HTML) from the drop-down menu.
- If it asks you if you want to Remove Office Tags, click Yes

If your book contains images, you'll need to create a compressed file to upload.

- Go to the folder where your book file is saved
- Right-click on the book file in the HTML format and select 'Send To' and then 'Compressed (zipped) folder'
- A new folder will appear. Drag your file into this zipped folder to upload into Kindle Direct Publishing (KDP)

That's it! You'll use this file to upload into KDP when you're ready to publish your book.

How to Format Your Book for Paperback Publishing

Formatting your book for paperback is just as easy as the process for Kindle formatting and will double your monthly sales. I'm always surprised how many people still want a paperback version even though the digital version costs half as much.

After formatting your book for paperback, you'll upload it to a print-on-demand service like CreateSpace or Lulu. I've uploaded some of my books to Lulu and Nook by Barnes & Noble but have never seen much in terms of sales so now I just stick with CreateSpace.

CreateSpace is owned by Amazon which means your paperback version will show as an option right next to the Kindle copy on your Amazon page. It's a great way to give potential readers a choice and reach more people.

- The main font for your book text should be 12-point Times New Roman. This shows up best after printing but other Serif-font forms will work also.
- Headings and chapter titles should be larger, at least 18-point font, and can be in a Sans Serif-font like Arial or Tahoma.

You'll want a one-inch margin at the top, bottom and sides just in case there are any errors in cutting the pages while printing and to make the book easier to read. You also want to leave a little space towards the center of the book where the pages come together. This is called the gutter and compensates for the space taken up by binding the pages together.

- Set your margins by clicking Layout in the menu then clicking on the arrow in the lower-right of the Page Setup tab
- In the box that appears, set your top/bottom/left/right margins to 0.9" and then 0.2" for the gutter
- Some word processing software has a checkbox for 'mirror margins' which needs to be checked to place the gutter on the left or right side depending on the page number

You also need to change the page size for the book. The most commonly used size is 6" by 9" for novels and non-fiction books.

- Click back to Layout in the menu and Page Setup. You can either click on Size or open up the dialog box by clicking on the arrow in the lower-right corner.
- Change the paper size drop-down to 'Custom Size' and change width to 6" and height to 9"
- Make sure the Portrait toggle is checked and click OK

There are some quirky rules for printing a book that you'll need to follow to make sure your book can be distributed as widely as possible.

- The number of pages must be a multiple of four to print out correctly. If you book isn't a multiple of 4 (does the number four fit into your total page numbers evenly, i.e. 76, 108,156,180) then you'll need to add a blank page or two somewhere.
- The last page should be blank on both sides for any markings from the retailer so this counts as two pages.
- The other side of the title page should be blank.
- The Table of Contents should begin on a right-side page

Just like proof reading your Kindle format, make sure you go through your paperback-formatted version before uploading it to CreateSpace or any other POD platform. It's a good idea to buy a proof copy of your book to review it in the printed form as well. Reviews are extremely important to your book's success and a poorly formatted book will destroy the reader experience.

How to Create a PDF Version of Your Book for Digital Sales

You'll also want a pdf or digital version of your book to email or use as a lead magnet for list subscribers. You can also use a pdf version to sell your book directly through your own website though I usually just link people to my Amazon page because those organic sales help keep your book ranked on the platform.

It takes all of a couple of mouse clicks to turn the Word version of your ebook into a pdf version.

1. Click File in the menu and then Save As
2. Make sure you are saving the document in the folder where you want it placed
3. Change the name of the file to '[Title] pdf version'
4. Click the drop-down arrow to change the file format to PDF and click Save

This will save a pdf version of your book and you'll still have the Word version to use as well.

More Tips on Book Formatting

Whether you follow the guide here for formatting your book or use another guide, you always need to check the finished book after it's been uploaded to Kindle, paperback or any other platform. Things sometimes get lost in translation and can damage your readers experience.

A few more tips on book formatting will help you avoid the most common problems with last minute changes.

- Use indentation instead of tabs or spaces to start paragraphs. Click on the Layout tab in the menu of Word and then the button at the lower-right corner of the Paragraph tab. This will open up a box to set your preferred indent numbers for the entire document and a special indent. Set Special to First line and 0.5 to indent your first line.

- Using the Return key after each paragraph doesn't always translate the space between paragraphs well in Kindle. Instead, change your spacing by going back to the Paragraph box you used to set indents and changing enter a value in the 'After' box of spacing. Most authors use 10-point spacing after a paragraph.
- Insert a page break between chapters to make sure each chapter starts on a new page. At the beginning of each chapter, click on Insert in the menu and then click Page Break in the left-most section.
- Insert images rather than using copy/paste. Place the cursor where you want the image to appear and click Insert in the menu. Then click Pictures which will bring up a folder you can use to find where the image is on your computer. Remember images are shown in shades of grey on Kindle so you may lose some detail for color images.
- Do not use headers or footers when formatting your book for Kindle. They will be lost.

How to get freelancers to format

I used freelancers to format most of my books until I learned how easy it was to do myself. Because it doesn't take that long, it's relatively cheap to hire someone out for the formatting. I paid $55 per book for most of my formatting which makes it something you can pay for if you just don't want to mess with one more detail.

Freelancers for formatting can be found easily on Upwork or Fiverr. Most of the gigs on Fiverr will start at $15 and limit your book to a certain number of pages and images so you'll have to pay extra for a regular-size book. Hiring someone directly from Upwork means they work more closely with you, messaging back and forth for changes.

Starting a project on Upwork is simple and takes less than five minutes. Making it as detailed as possible, including bullet points for steps or deliverables, will avoid any confusion later.

Freelancers will bid on your project, usually with a bid that's pretty close to the fixed amount you say you want to pay. You can look at freelancer's past work and reviews and arrange for a phone interview.

When the freelancer submits the formatted versions of your book, make sure you review each for errors and mistakes. Spaces between words and paragraphs have a way of disappearing, sometimes at the fault of the freelancer and sometimes because Microsoft Word makes the changes.

Read through each formatted copy one more time and run the spell check. This is normally what a Proof Editor would do, checking the final 'proof' versions of the book, but there's no reason you can't do it yourself and save a little money. If you're sending out pre-release copies of your book to friends for review, you can also ask them to keep an eye out for mistakes.

After formatting a few of your books, it will become so easy that you can do it in less than 30 minutes. A lot of the formatting, you'll remember to do while writing and won't have to go back to fix afterwards.

Formatting your book for Kindle and other versions is one of those tasks that seem a lot more difficult than it is. It's really no more than changing a few settings in your word processor software and going back through to make some changes after you're done writing. You can hire a freelancer for book formatting but it pays to learn the process if you're going to be self-publishing more than a couple of books.

How to Create an Audiobook

Audiobook versions of your self-published books are easy to make and can lead to a big increase in income.

If there is one market in the self-publishing space that is still easier to compete in, it's within audiobooks. There are more than four million ebooks and paperbacks available on Amazon but less than 200,000 audiobooks on Audible.

That means your self-published audiobook is going to rank higher and get more sales.

Across my ten books, I make almost a third of my sales from audio versions. I average 140 audiobook copies sold each month and average three bounties.

Yeah, those bounties are when someone downloads your book as part of their free trial on Audible and it's worth an extra $50 payout…so, Ka-ching!

Creating an audiobook version isn't nearly as difficult as you might think for a solid revenue source. I'm going to walk you through how to get your book ready for recording, how to record and how to get it published.

How to Get Your Book Ready for Recording

The first thing you'll need to do to get your book ready is to read through it and reword for audio listeners. This includes changing references from pages and graphics to descriptions.

- Change any reference to page location, i.e. 'on the next page'
- Change any reference to visual cues, i.e. 'you'll see here'

- Remove graphics
- Remove the table of contents and glossary
- If there are any long lists or bulleted points in your book, you'll need to rewrite these sections

The hardest part of this will be describing the information you had in images and charts. If a picture is worth a thousand words, does that mean you need to add 1,000 words of description for each image removed? Ok, not so much.

You'll also need to read through the book for conversational tone and readability. Hopefully there aren't too many awkward sentences but there is a difference between seeing a sentence as a reader and hearing it in an audiobook.

It's a good idea to break up any long paragraphs of more than three or four sentences. Any more than this and it's going to sound like you're droning on in the recording. You want to give your listeners the material in short, manageable chunks.

There is also some Audible required content you'll need to add to the book.

Audiobooks must include opening and closing credits that include title, author, narrator and copyright information. There are specific words you need to say so I wouldn't stray too much from the script Audible provides.

Your opening credits will be, "This is the audiobook version of [Title]. Written and narrated by [Name]."

Your closing credits will be, "This has been the audiobook version of [Title]. Written and narrated by [Name]. Copyright [Year] by [Your Company]. Production copyright [Year]. The End."

These are pretty easy to add as the first and last things you say when you go to record your book.

During your recording, each chapter must start with the narrator saying the chapter number and chapter title. It's a good idea to spell this out at the beginning of each chapter in your script so you don't forget.

Do You Need to Use a Recording Studio for Your Audiobook?

You don't necessarily need to record your audiobook in a professional studio but it could save you a lot of time. Audible is strict about sound quality and background noises are the most common reason recordings get rejected.

Something as minor as the buzz of a ceiling fan or air conditioning can come through in your recordings and you'll have to record again. There are ways to prepare a room in your home for quality recording which we'll cover later in the article.

The cost for studio time will vary depending on where you live. You can time your speaking speed to get an idea of how much time it will take to record your book. Normal speaking speed is around 150 words per minute which means a 35,000-word book will just under four hours.

In all but the largest cities, studio time will usually cost between $35 to $75 per hour. That may include some post-production editing and mastering but make sure you ask. If it's not included, sound engineers usually cost around the same range per finished hour of recording.

A general rule of thumb is that recording and post-production editing for an audiobook costs around $75 to $150 per finished hour of recording but there are ways to discount this price.

- If you're using a studio, try negotiating a lower rate to add the engineer's time for post-production editing.

- You can find experienced sound engineers on Upwork for $35 an hour
- Learn post-production mastering through a course on Udemy for as little as $20 and save hundreds

Don't skimp too much on quality just to save a couple hundred dollars. Not only will poor quality recordings get rejected by Audible, requiring more time on your part, but readers will hit you hard in the reviews.

Audiobook Recording Requirements

Before we talk about recording your audiobook and how to do it in your own home, let's go over a few of the technical requirements from Audible.

- Recordings must be in a WAV format at 44.1 kHz
- Set the recording for a peak of -6 dB and a maximum noise floor of -60 dB
- Set the RMS recording between -23 dB and -18 dB
- Record everything in either all mono or all stereo but not in both
- Read each chapter number and title on each section and leave about two seconds of empty space before you start talking and at the end of the section
- Each audio file must contain only one chapter and be shorter than 120 minutes
- Transfer the WAV files to a MP3 format in 192 kbps or higher and at a constant bit rate

Professional recording software such as Audacity will make it relatively easy to set up these criteria but it's also nice to have a professional do it for you. You can get a lot of help on your audiobook for less than $500 and save yourself a lot of time. At an average income around $50 per audiobook each month, you can make up those costs quickly.

One audiobook hack to consider, plan your next vacation to somewhere with less expensive studio and engineer costs. You'll save hundreds on recording and can write off part of your trip as a business expense.

Should You Record Your Own Audiobook?

This is one of the first questions I get when talking to people about audiobooks.

The rule of thumb is that you should narrate your own non-fiction books. You know the material better than anyone and are going to be the most enthusiastic reading it. Your listeners will pick up on your passion and enthusiasm and that will go a long way in holding their attention.

Having someone else narrate your non-fiction book might be an option if you can find someone with very high authority or popularity in the topic. The problem is that unless they are a personal friend or family member, the cost is probably not going to be worth it.

For fictional stories, you'll need voice actors to bring the characters to life. Audible has a network of voice actors you can hire or you can also find them through talent agencies. If you can get your friends and family excited about the roles, you might be able to get them to record a few parts and save yourself a lot of money.

Equipment to Record an Audiobook at Home

Creating an audiobook from home is easily doable. It might mean several hours more learning how to set up and use your equipment then post-production mastering but it will also save you several hundred dollars.

You'll first need some basic tools and equipment for the recording and mastering.

- Computer with at least one USB port
- Blue Yeti or ATR 2100 series microphone with pop filter
- Audacity software for PC or Garageband software for Mac
- Digital tablet

A pop filter is that cloth piece that you see in front of microphones when someone is doing a professional recording. Without it, you'll get loud bursts of air whenever you make a p- or b-sound.

You'll need to record in a room smaller than 20x20 but preferably as small as 6x6 with carpet. A large, empty room will cause an echo that might not be noticeable talking but will show up in your recording. Carpet helps to absorb those bouncing sound waves and it's a good idea to cover the walls with blankets if you can.

If the room is especially large or empty, try bringing in furniture to absorb the echo. A couch and recliners work well for this and can make a big difference in your recording. If your room has a window with recurring outside noises, you might need to record late at night when there won't be as many distractions.

You'll want to set up your microphone so your mouth is no farther than six or eight inches at all times. Try staying a consistent distance from the mic while recording so the volume stays at the same level.

Test speaking into the mic at your normal volume. You'll see the recording rise and fall as you speak and most recording software will include a decibel scale. Adjust the recording level of your microphone so that the spikes when you're speaking fall between -24 and -12 DB. This will keep your recording from 'peaking' - reaching all the way to 0, but will also allow you to increase the volume if you need to without worrying about the sound floor.

Use a digital tablet with your script so you can scroll with your finger instead of having to click keys on the laptop or turn pages. These noises will be picked up in recording and Audible will reject your files. Don't forget to turn off WiFi so incoming messages and beeps don't disturb your recording.

Tips on Recording Your Audiobook at Home

While you're recording, don't stop after a mistake. Snap your fingers or cough, leave a couple seconds of space and then start back to the last paragraph. This will save recording time and you can go back to edit out the mistake. You'll see a spike in the recording where you coughed and then no sound which will tip you off to where your mistakes are when you're editing.

The opening and closing credits should be their own files. Each chapter should also be recorded as a separate file.

Audible requires a few seconds of room tone at the beginning and end of each file. This means letting the recording run a second or two before you start talking and after your final word in each chapter. If you miss recording on a chapter or two, you can record the room tone separately and then just add it to your file but it's easier to do it all at once.

Plan on spending from two to three hours of recording and post-recording production for every hour of finished audio. Normal out-loud reading speed is around 150 words per minute and you'll spend an hour or two editing and mastering the recorded clips.

Narrating your audiobook is one-part conversation with your listeners and one part acting. You can't just read through your book. Holding your listeners' attention means getting excited and letting that through in your reading. It may seem like you're being overly dramatic but read your book with more emotion than your normal conversational tone.

You'll be surprised how much the recording takes out of you. Have some tea ready for a drink or two between chapters to soothe your voice. If you're recording more than four hours, take a break and consider breaking up anything more than six hours into two days.

Uploading Your Audiobook into Audible for Self-Publishing

Uploading your converted files to Audible is the easy part. Remember, you'll need to convert the files to MP3 format at 192 kb per second or higher and at a constant bit rate or Audible won't accept them.

You'll upload your opening and closing credits and each chapter separately. You'll also need to upload a retail sample of up to five minutes for potential customers to listen before they buy. I usually just use my introduction chapter for this since it contains a good mix of information and sales copy for the book.

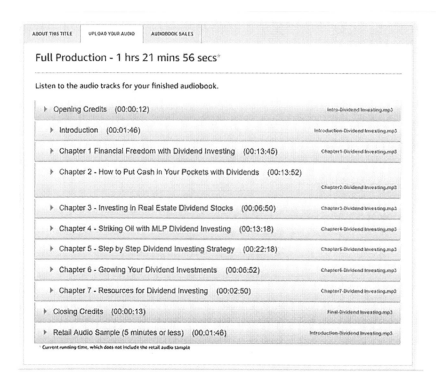

Full Production - 1 hrs 21 mins 56 secs*

Listen to the audio tracks for your finished audiobook.

▶ Opening Credits (00:00:12)   Intro-Dividend Investing.mp3

▶ Introduction (00:01:46)   Introduction-Dividend Investing.mp3

▶ Chapter 1 Financial Freedom with Dividend Investing (00:13:45)   Chapter1-Dividend Investing.mp3

▶ Chapter 2 - How to Put Cash In Your Pockets with Dividends (00:13:52)
                                                                                 Chapter2-Dividend Investing.mp3

▶ Chapter 3 - Investing in Real Estate Dividend Stocks (00:06:50)   Chapter3-Dividend Investing.mp3

▶ Chapter 4 - Striking Oil with MLP Dividend Investing (00:13:18)   Chapter4-Dividend Investing.mp3

▶ Chapter 5 - Step by Step Dividend Investing Strategy (00:22:18)   Chapter5-Dividend Investing.mp3

▶ Chapter 6 - Growing Your Dividend Investments (00:06:52)   Chapter6-Dividend Investing.mp3

▶ Chapter 7 - Resources for Dividend Investing (00:02:50)   Chapter7-Dividend Investing.mp3

▶ Closing Credits (00:00:13)   Final-Dividend Investing.mp3

▶ Retail Audio Sample (5 minutes or less) (00:01:46)   Introduction-Dividend Investing.mp3

* Current running time, which does not include the retail audio sample

Unlike Kindle and paperback publishing, you won't set the price for your audiobook. Audible automatically sets the price based on the length of the recording.

- Books under an hour long are generally $7 or less
- 1 – 3 hours: $7 to $10
- 3 – 5 hours: $10 to $20
- 5 – 10 hours: $15 to $25
- 10 – 20 hours: $20 to $30

It usually takes between four and six days for your book to show up on Audible and another few days to get listed on your Amazon sales page. How much you receive generally depends on how the book is bought through different promotions.

- AL – An Audible member purchases your book with credits they receive as part of their monthly subscription.

- ALOP – An Audible member purchases your book without credits but at the standard 30% discount on the retail price.
- ALC – A retail purchase of your book, usually through iTunes or Amazon.

The amount the customer pays varies depending on how they buy your book but you will receive 40% of the price paid. That usually means between $2.50 to $4.50 per copy sold.

Audiobook Cover Requirements

One last note but an important one. Audible has specific requirements for the cover image on your book.

- Images must be no smaller than 2400 X 2400 pixels in size.
- The resolution of these images can be no smaller than 72 dpi.
- Images must be squared. The squared cover must be a true squared cover and cannot be rectangular with colored borders on the side.
- Images should be at least 24-bit.
- Image types allowed: JPEG, TIFF, PNG
- Images must contain both the name of the title and author(s)

This means you'll need to rework your standard book design into something that will fit a square format. Resist the urge to just make the design fit the new layout. Remember, people will judge your book by its cover.

Creating an audiobook is a long process but you're creating an asset that will generate income for you every month. There are a lot of people that enjoy audiobooks over digital or paperback formats and you need to reach that market. Once you create an audiobook, the process will become much faster and easier for later books so don't let the time keep you from taking advantage of this great income source.

How to Create a $10,000 Amazon Book Description [Case Study]

Putting together an awesome Amazon book description is easy and will mean consistent sales

I spent weeks getting ready to launch my first self-published book in March 2015. I researched how to launch a book, how to get reviews and how to create an Amazon book description that could get people to buy.

In the 30 months since, the book has sold more than 3,800 copies on Kindle, paperback and audible. It's made over $10,000 and stays consistently on the first page of search results in several categories.

It's obviously not the only book on Amazon about crowdfunding. There are thousands available and that's not even counting related books on non-profit fundraising and small business funding.

How does my book stay in the top ten within the crowdfunding and the non-profits categories? How does it consistently sell over 100 copies a month?

Of all the things I did before launching, I think it was learning how to create an interesting and persuasive book description that has made the most difference.

A great book description will not only convert window shoppers into buyers but it will also get you enough purchases that your book will stay consistently ranked.

I'm going to walk you through the seven critical parts of your Amazon book description and how to set it up.

Parts of an Amazon Book Description Page

I want to point out each of the most important parts on your Amazon page first and then we'll walk through each to see how you can set it up.

So here is a screenshot of my book page for Step-by-Step Crowdfunding.

I've removed the 'People also Read' and 'Sponsored products related to this item' sections for length. These sections come just under the book description and will draw people away from your book if you don't have a rock-solid cover, title and description.

The **cover** is the first thing people see when they click through to your book. It has to be interesting and professional-quality.

Amazon makes the **book title and subtitle** bolded and in very large font so it's going to always be something that stands out to anyone visiting your page. It's also very important for showing up in different searches.

The **number of reviews and stars** you get on your book don't affect your search ranking directly but are extremely important for converting people into buyers. We'll cover more about how to get great reviews in an upcoming book launch article.

You absolutely need at least Kindle and paperback **formats for your book**. You can format your book for both in less than an hour and will reach more people. I would go a step further and say you also need an audio version of your book. It's super easy to create an audiobook and there is much less competition.

Some people only read on Kindle, some still like getting a paperback copy. Other people listen to audiobooks in their car or wherever. Don't lose easy sales because you didn't take a little extra time to reach as many potential buyers as possible.

The **book description** is way more important than most authors understand. Not only will it persuade people to buy your book but it's also important in getting ranked for different searches on Amazon. We'll spend most of the next section setting up an amazing book description.

People can scroll down to check out the reviews of your book but why not show them the best reviews first? The **editorial reviews section** is your chance to really highlight some great reviews from notable readers.

The **From the Author section** is your last chance to reach potential readers on a personal level, tell them why you wrote the book and how it will help them.

Creating Your Amazon Book Page for Massive Sales

I'm doing separate articles for cover design, creating different book formats and getting reviews for your self-published book. Picking your keywords and book categories is also extremely important, so important I'll be doing a separate article for those as well.

We'll spend the rest of this article in a step-by-step to creating a title, description, editorial reviews and author section that will make your book a success.

Some of these can be done on the Amazon Direct Publishing platform (ADP), other parts are done on the Amazon Author Central website. The ADP platform is where you will fill out title, description, publishing info, price and will upload your files. Author Central is a separate website where you can track your author rank, customer reviews and set up more page information for each book.

The first thing you'll do when you go to publish your book on Amazon is to put in the title. Amazon allows you to have a title and sub-title. Your title needs to be exactly what is printed on your book but your sub-title can be longer and include more than the official sub-title.

This is important because your title and sub-title are big factors in how Amazon ranks your book for different keywords. When someone does a search on Amazon, you want your book to show up if its relevant, right?

So your title should be persuasive and include your biggest keyword target, something with a high number of monthly searches on Amazon. Use your sub-title to get in maybe one or two more keywords but also to include other persuasive content through adjectives and a sense of urgency through time-related words.

Some points to consider for your sub-title:

- People love numbered lists, i.e. 10 ways to…
- Boost your credibility with words like 'proven' and 'experts'
- Create a sense of urgency or a time-related promise with words like 'now', 'fast' or 'in 30 days'
- Use emotional triggers like curiosity, amazement or uncertainty

Of course, your title and sub-title need to be relevant to your book and you have to deliver on any promises made. Kindle readers can easily return a book so you can't just hook them with a catchy title and then give them a crappy book.

This is going to apply to your entire Amazon book page but especially the title, don't do everything in one sitting. Don't just work through these pieces once and create your page.

- Brainstorm at least 10 title and sub-title ideas after looking through some of the highest-ranking books already on Amazon
- Give it a day and come back to your ideas, narrowing it down to a few
- Test out your title ideas in Facebook, asking people to vote on the most interesting

Writing an Awesome Book Description

Amazon let's you use up to 4,000 characters for your book description. That's about 600 – 700 words.

Use every - single - last - word possible!

There are a lot of opportunities for people to click away from your book page before buying. From sponsored books to ads and 'people also read' suggestions, you need to use every opportunity you can to convince people why your book is worth their time and money.

Your book description is also critical for letting Amazon know how to rank your book in keyword searches. Besides an ecommerce platform, Amazon is also a search platform and billions of searches are conducted every month. You want your book to show up in those searches, right?

Well then you need to learn how to use your book description for search.

So, let's walk through the important parts of your book description and how to set each up.

First, you'll need to use an html converter on a website outside of Amazon. HTML is the computer language that tells Amazon how to highlight, bold and bullet your description. The box you see on the Amazon Direct Publishing page for your description will take that HTML.

A note here, you can also use Author Central to put in your book description but it the HTML won't work. You want to use the description box in ADP.

Finding an html converter is easy, just do a google search for 'Amazon description html editor'. These will let you write in your description, add formatting and H-tags and then it will create the html code to copy to your ADP page.

Writing your description, you want a good balance of information and sales pitch. You're not just telling potential readers what the book is about but what it means for them, what they'll get out of it.

Remember this rule in marketing,

People don't buy products, they buy the transformation.

That means, anytime you are writing to persuade someone, you need to figure out what the product will do for them and write to that. How will the information in the book change their lives? What will it help them do?

While you're doing this, you want to make sure you hit some key items in your description.

Main headline - You'll write one sentence that will be a main headline and make it an H1 or H2 tag in the HTML editor. This is the first thing people will see in your description and has to catch their interest.

Irresistible questions or transformational promises work best. That means ask them a question they can't resist knowing the answer to or grab them with the hope of an aspirational transformation.

Bulleted topics and page numbers - I love this book description tactic. You pick four or five really great references from the book, a few things readers will be super-excited to see, and make a bullet list. Adding the page numbers where they'll find the information makes it more than just a sales pitch but guarantees that it's in the book waiting for them.

Section headings - Nobody wants to read one long block of text. Break up your book description into sections just like you would a blog post or story. Like the headline, these section headings should include some of the keywords for which you want to rank on Amazon. Section headings should be marked as an H-tag in your HTML editor, usually one less than your headline either an H2 or H3.

Multiple Calls to Action (CTA) - At least twice in your description, have a sentence that tells readers to 'scroll up and click buy'. It's too easy for readers to just read through a book description and then keep reading down the page.

The problem for authors is that just below the description is two rows of advertising for other books on Amazon. Grab potential readers with your description and tell them how to start their transformation, by scrolling back up and clicking buy now.

Common questions and keywords - You want to be answering common reader questions and using keywords throughout your book description. Answering common questions your readers have will help potential buyers see that you know what they need and have the answers.

Using keywords is a must when trying to rank on Amazon. You don't have to stuff your keywords in the description. You'll naturally be using the words when writing about the subject anyway. Try writing up your description first and then going back through to replace a few words with keywords where they fit.

Your Last Chance to Hook Potential Readers with Your Amazon Page

If you're not able to hook readers with your description, you still have a couple of sections to grab them.

Through your pre-launch marketing to friends and connections in the book's topic, you need to line up a few people that will review your book. This means you'll send them a draft copy before publishing which they can use to leave a review once your Amazon page is live.

I'll cover more about the launch in a coming article but these people are part of your launch team, helping to spread the word and get reviews.

Ask a few of these people if they can email their reviews before launch to put in your **Editorial Reviews** section of the page. As opposed to the other parts of your page, you'll use your Author Central account to create this section.

Preferably, editorial reviews should come from other experts in the topic. It might be difficult to find someone with name recognition to be on your launch team but that's what you want. These reviews not only help you demonstrate social proof, that other people have read the book, but you can curate the section so potential buyers see only the best reviews.

The last section I usually use for my Amazon book pages is the **From the Author** note. This is also done through your Author Central account.

The 'From the Author' section is your chance to reach people on a personal level. Connect with them and show them you're not just trying to sell a book. Talk about what the information in the book did for you and why you're so excited about sharing it with others. This is your last chance to talk about the transformation that will convince readers to buy your book.

Key Points to Consider for Your Amazon Book Page

I see so many authors spend months making a great book and then try to rush through their book description page. I know the feeling when you've spent so long working on a book and just want to launch as soon as possible.

Resist the temptation to skim over these last crucial pieces in your self-publishing journey. Thousands of people a month are going to be coming to your Amazon book page. You want to convert as many as possible to readers and the only way to do that is through a great book description.

- Strategically plan your title and sub-title to grab readers' attentions and include important keywords
- Write out a full description that not only excites readers but also shows Amazon the keywords for which you want to rank
- Focus on the transformation rather than the information. People aren't buying your knowledge, they're buying what it will help them become.
- Within your description, include a headline, section headings, bulleted list, calls-to-action, and keywords
- Work on getting a few big-name influencers to help you with a review for your editorial reviews section
- Reach people on a personal level within the From the Author section

Creating a great Amazon book description page doesn't happen overnight, it shouldn't anyway. Write through the sections but spend a few days coming back and reviewing until everything's perfect. A strong book page will convert readers for consistent sales, helping you stay ranked in your categories after your launch. That's how I sell hundreds of copies a month for each of my books and your best bet for success.

Picking Perfect Amazon Categories and Keywords for Sales

Break the Amazon best-seller code by balancing popularity and competition with your categories and keywords

Part of self-publishing a book on Amazon is putting together a page, picking categories for your book and helping the ecommerce giant understand your book by selecting keywords that relate to the content.

These decisions all seem like they should be obvious and easy. Simply selecting the most appropriate category and describing your book a little.

If it seems easy, then you're probably not doing it right!

Picking the right categories can mean the difference between your book ranking consistently and making sales or just being another of the four million books available on Kindle.

Yeah, it's that important.

You're allowed to pick two categories in which your book will rank to show when people browse on Amazon. Of my 10 books, so 20 categories, I rank on the first page consistently in 14 of those categories.

Keywords are also hugely important in all this because it's how readers find your book when searching on Amazon and Google.

I'm going to show you my process for picking perfect categories and then how you can find undiscovered keywords that will lead people straight to your book.

How to Win the Amazon Book Category Game

When you're doing a Google search or browsing a category on Amazon, how often do you click past the first page of results?

Never? Maybe rarely?

In self-publishing as it is in a lot of things, if you're not in that first group of books recommended, you're not going to be successful.

There are 32 top-level categories for books on Amazon, as many as a couple dozen sub-categories within each and a few tertiary categories even within each of these sub-categories.

When someone is looking for a book to read, they either do a keyword search or they'll just start browsing categories. Sometimes, even if they start with a keyword search, they'll end up clicking through in the left-side menu and start browsing categories.

The problem is that even some of the sub-categories on Amazon are extremely difficult to rank your book consistently in the top 10 or 20, that first page.

Tony Robbins' Money Master the Game book has over 2,600 reviews with an average 4 ½ stars ranking. It's ranked #10,800 on Kindle right now which means he's probably selling around 25 to 30 a day minimum...and it's ranked sixty-ninth in the Motivational sub-category of self-help.

Tony Robbins, motivational guru that sells out stadiums for his seminars is stuck on the third page of Amazon in his category.

The lesson, don't stick your book in the Motivational sub-category.

There is a game you have to play here. You need to find a category that is appropriate to your book. No sense showing a self-help book to people browsing in art history, right? But you also need to find a category in which you can actually rank on the first page. No sense in having your book buried on the third page if nobody is going to see it.

So there's a tradeoff here, finding a sub-category for your book that will show it to targeted readers but is not so competitive that they never see it while browsing.

How to Pick an Amazon Category for Your Self-Published Book

Amazon used to make it easier to pick a category for your book. In the past, browsing through the categories, you could see displayed next to the category how many books were published in each. This would give you an idea of how competitive each category was going to be.

Amazon took those numbers away so now you have to go a little deeper to find your perfect book category.

The first thing you will do is select Kindle Store in the drop-down search menu and click the magnifying glass. This will show you only Kindle books and you can browse through the list of categories in the left-side menu.

Note down which of the 32 categories even remotely have anything to do with your book. Then click through each and do the same within the sub-categories. So you're going to be creating something like a pyramid chart with the relevant categories on top then lines down from each of those to the sub-categories relevant to your book and lines down from each of those to the tertiary categories.

You want to find every possible category path where you could realistically put your book in to show it to targeted readers.

For example, I started doing this for a motivational book. Among the top-level categories, it might fit in Health, Fitness & Dating or Business & Money or Parenting & Relationships. Click through the Business & Money category and it might fit in the Management & Leadership or the Entrepreneurship sub-category. Clicking through those, you see that it might fit in the Leadership, Management or the Motivational tertiary categories.

You do that for every category through sub-category in the list.

If you click all the way through to the final point in each path, to a sub-category or tertiary level and then scroll down, you will see a number count for how many books are in that group. So for the Leadership group of the Management & Leadership sub-category, we see that there are 34,937 books competing for ranking in this space...tough.

Do this for all the paths in your chart, noting how many books are in that group. We see that there are only 5,816 books in the Men's Health group of the Health & Fitness category so that might be an idea.

We're not quite done yet though.

As you're working through each category path and you scroll down to see how many books are in that category, click through the top 10 books in each. So now you're on a book page and you want to scroll down to where it says Product Details.

Write down the Amazon Best-Sellers Rank for each of the top ten books. Add them all up and then divide by 10 for the average. You should also note the rank of the tenth book in the category to see where you will need to rank to break that top ten spot.

The best-sellers rank is determined by how many copies of a book are sold each month. So we can get a rough estimate for how competitive a category is, how hard it will be to rank your book in the top ten.

Sales per day needed to rank on best-seller list:

- < 10,000 26 sales daily or about 390 a month
- 10,000 to 25,000 10 sales or about 157 a month
- 25,000 to 50,000 5 sales or about 76 a month
- 50,000 to 100,000 2 sales a day or about 35 per month

Now these aren't exact numbers but the result of many, many authors sharing their sales and ranking information so it's a good rule of thumb.

Notice multiplying daily sales needed for rank is more than that needed in a month. This is because Amazon weights recent sales more than monthly sales so if you can promote your book and get a few days of consistently high sales then can boost your rank. Amazon does use monthly sales though so longer-term sales is important and you can't just have a quick burst of sales followed by nothing.

Selling more than five books a day may not sound too difficult but it is. Besides a marketing strategy with Amazon ads, you're going to need some major traffic from your own website to break into the top 25,000 books.

Your sweet spot for a category is if you can find one where the tenth book is ranked between 50,000 to 100,000 on the best-sellers list. This is doable and you should be able to sell enough books consistently to rank well in this category.

Now if you're name is Oprah (first off, Hi Oprah - big fan) then you'll have a shot at the much more competitive categories because you can rank in that top 10,000 consistently. For the rest of us, be realistic about how many books you can sell each month and what kind of rank you can hold.

A note here, you can change your category after the book is published so this isn't set in stone. Check your category ranking every few months for that first year after publication. Change to a more less competitive category if you aren't holding your own or maybe even to a more popular category if you find you can compete at a higher level.

Beyond just the objective research for each category, check out the Amazon pages for each book in the top ten within potential categories. Read through the descriptions and reviews. Look at the covers. Can you beat them? Can you write compelling descriptions and is your cover something that is going to stand out?

Watch out for the number of reviews for each book in the top ten or twenty. If most of the books ranking on the first page of a category have hundreds or even thousands of reviews, how are you going to beat that?

One last note here, when you're doing your category research, books priced at $0.99 are probably on promotion so may not be representative of the top-ranking books in the category. These books might have gotten a quick boost but might not stay in the rankings.

Finding Secret Categories for Your Self-Published Book

Beyond the categories you can choose for your book when you upload the files into Kindle Direct Publishing, there are some secret categories for which you can rank if they are appropriate to your book.

These secret categories are ones for which you have to contact Amazon for inclusion and you need to have specific keywords in your description or title to qualify. I guess Amazon has gotten tired of people trying to cram their book into these categories so it requires this second-level of verification.

Amazon lists these categories, along with the secret categories we'll get to, on its KDP help topics page 'Selecting Browse Categories'.

Why would you want to go through the trouble of getting added to one of these categories? Because they are much less competitive than the easier ones to select.

Click through to each of the categories that might be relevant to your book and you'll see sub-categories and the relevant keywords that must be included.

It's a little more difficult researching these categories because they don't show in the left-side menu of Amazon automatically. You have to find a book in the category and then click through in the Product Details section to browse the list of books. Then you can see how well the books in the category do and whether you might have a chance to compete.

If you want to try one of these secret categories, first add the relevant keywords as one of your seven keywords when you create the book in the Kindle Direct Publishing platform. You can change your keywords so don't worry if you created your book with different keywords.

Then it's just a matter of contacting Amazon to request your book be put in the category.

Go to the contact-us page in your Author Central account. On the contact form, select My Books and Update Information About a Book within the details drop-down menu. Select Browse Categories and "I want to browse categories in the Product Details section in the last drop-down menu.

Provide your book's ASIN number which is the ten-digit number in your book URL on Amazon or also available in the product details section. Also provide the browsing path to the restricted category, starting with Kindle Store>Kindle eBooks>...

Amazon is usually quick to respond within 24 hours and will change your book's category.

Why are Keywords Important for Your Amazon Book?

When you create your book in Kindle Direct Publishing, you are allowed to pick up to seven keywords or phrases for which your book will rank when people search. These are not the only keywords for which your book will rank but this is telling Amazon that these phrases are especially relevant and your book should show when someone is looking for them.

Like Google, Amazon is a search engine. Millions of people use it to search for books every day and millions more come from Google search directly to books because of the keywords they use.

The keywords you select for your book are important not only for these seven spots but you're also going to want to use them within your book description and sub-title. That is going to help your book show up on Google search and on Amazon.

So you've got another tradeoff here with your keywords. You can write down something like 'Making Money' which gets hundreds of thousands of searches a month but for which you'll probably never rank in the top ten or 20 books. You can select something like 'making money on Mars' which has just four books ranking for the keyword...but probably even fewer people looking for it.

How to Find the Best Keywords for Your Book

Finding the best keywords for your book is a lot like the keyword research you'll do if you want to rank a blog post on Google. I'm going to show you a process for finding keywords that will bring lots of traffic to your book but with less competition.

A note first about some keywords you don't want to use.

- Your title should be your main target keyword but you don't have to include that in the seven you choose in KDP. Your book will automatically rank for the words in your title because Amazon assumes that's what it's about.
- Don't include qualifiers like 'best' or 'top' in your keywords
- Don't include price information or adjectives like 'new' or 'sale' in your keywords

Using adjectives like 'best' in your keywords to rank a blog post on Google is a good idea but won't help you on Amazon.

First, brainstorm a general list of keyword phrases that relate to your book. You should be able to put together a list of 10 to 20 words that relate to your book's topic. Just put yourself in the reader's shoes. What search terms would you use if you were trying to solve the problems addressed in your book?

With this list, go to the Amazon search bar. Change the department to Kindle and start searching for your list of ideas, one-by-one.

Notice that Amazon auto-populates your search with suggestions in the drop-down. For example, if I start typing 'Making Money' then it starts suggesting searches like 'making money online' and 'making money from home'.

These are searches related to what you are typing in their order of popularity. It's a great way of finding keywords related to a major idea but maybe that aren't as competitive.

Make sure you open your internet browser (Firefox, Chrome, etc) in incognito mode. This disables cookies placed on your computer from websites. Amazon uses cookies, little tracking codes, to see what you have looked for in the past and to suggest personalized search results.

Since you don't want search suggestions based on your past behavior, you want to turn these off by using incognito mode so Amazon will just suggest searches based on traffic.

Add to your list, all the search suggestions you get from Amazon for each of your first list.

Then use this same process on Google. When you search on Google, it will not only start suggesting searches but will also tell you what other searches people used if you scroll down to the bottom of the page.

A super-sneaky way to find great keywords is to steal them from other websites. Search for a few of your keywords in Google and copy the web address for the first two or three results.

Then go to Ahrefs.com and paste one of the addresses in the search bar for its site explorer. Click on 'Organic Keywords' in the left-side menu and you'll see all the keywords for which that page ranks.

Filter this page for ranking from zero to 20 and then export them into a spreadsheet. You'll need a subscription to do this but the site offers a 14-day free trial and you can get everything done before having to pay.

After you've done this with a few pages that rank highly for your keyword ideas, combine all the spreadsheets. You'll see a column labeled 'Volume' and another one labeled KD or keyword difficulty. This KD is an estimate of how difficult it is to rank on Google for that keyword.

Put in an equation in a new column dividing volume by KD to give you a measure of how difficult it is to rank keywords with the highest volume of monthly searches. You can sort the spreadsheet for this column, from largest to smallest, to find the easiest keywords with the highest search popularity.

You can also plug your other keyword ideas into the Ahrefs' keyword explorer to find search volume and difficulty to add to your list.

Now Google search isn't exactly the same as Amazon search traffic but they're pretty close. Keywords that get a lot of traffic on Google are also likely to get a lot on Amazon.

Just from those few steps, you should have a list of keyword ideas approaching 100 from which to choose seven. Search on Amazon for each and note how many books show up in the search, this is given in the upper-left side of the screen.

Narrow the list down a little, say to 50 potential keyword ideas, and find the average best-seller rank of the top ten books. Check out the number of reviews and quality of the book covers.

Take your time because reader searches are a huge driver of traffic on Amazon. You want to pick the very best keywords for which you can rank. Balancing between search volume and competition with books in the search, measured by best-seller rank and other factors, will help you find your seven perfect keywords.

Picking categories and keywords for your self-published books on Amazon is more important than most authors understand and will go a long way to helping push consistent monthly sales. It can be a long process of research but it's all part of the business of using Amazon to sell your books. Remember, Amazon is just a computer so it runs on rules. Learn how to take advantage of these rules and your book will be an instant success.

Book Launch Blueprint: Step-by-Step to a Best-selling Launch

A book launch strategy will protect your Amazon rankings and turn your book into a best-seller

I bet you thought writing a great book was all it took to be a successful author. If that were only the case.

There are so many books available online and in print that it takes much more to consistently sell books. It takes a best-selling book launch strategy.

A book launch strategy for each book I self-publish is how I consistently rank as one of the top authors in the Business & Money category on Amazon. It may not seem like much, ranking 285th among authors in the category or around 9,800[th] overall but that's among more than a million authors.

It also means I consistently sell over 600 copies and earn just under $2,000 each month.

A book launch strategy is one of the most important pieces of the self-publishing puzzle but also one of the most often neglected. It takes months to write, edit and format a book. By the time you have a final copy ready, you'll be so eager to publish that you'll be tempted to rush through the launch.

But a good launch will make all the difference in how well your book does after the first few weeks.

The majority of books on Amazon make money for just a couple of weeks when first published, as the author's friends and family buy copies. After that, rankings plunge and nobody ever sees it again while browsing.

It is very difficult to get a book's rankings back up after it has fallen below #300,000 or so on the best-sellers' list. You'll have wasted whatever momentum you had in the first couple of weeks and will have to start from scratch with a new launch.

Do yourself a favor. Use this book launch blueprint to jumpstart your Amazon book ranking and cement your book's position.

Why is a Book Launch So Important?

A good book launch will make your self-published books nearly completely passive as an income source. I spend about $20 per book each month on Amazon ads, which are completely automated, and get some sales from blog readers but almost all my sales are from Amazon.

The hundreds of sales I get from Amazon are because each book is launched to jumpstart the ranking process.

You see, if you can jumpstart Amazon's ranking program for your books then the world's largest shopping site will take over and sell your books for you.

The problem with most book launches is that they fizzle out after a few days. The way Amazon ranks books and products is on one-month sales so having a few days of high sales may boost your book to #1 but it won't keep it there.

A successful launch sells your book over a couple of weeks to really cement your rankings. After a couple of weeks of strong sales, even a few days of lower sales won't ruin your book's ranking. From there, people are going to consistently see your book in search and in the 'best of' pages for the categories and you'll get enough sales to keep your rankings.

Your launch is also important to create social proof through reviews. Amazon says reviews don't directly affect how it ranks your book, but they certainly affect rankings indirectly.

One of the first things a reader will see, whether it's browsing through Amazon search results or a category page, is the number of reviews and average stars rating. These are hard to miss, contrasting with the rest of the page in bright yellow.

Social proof is the idea that people trust the 'wisdom of the crowd'. If you see that lots of other people are doing or buying something, it's something you're more likely to do or buy.

It's almost instinctual, right? There's safety in numbers.

Of the 2.1 million books available on Kindle, 78% are rated four-stars or higher. Another 16% are rated three-stars and the remaining 6% have just one- or two-star ratings.

Any book with less than a four-star average is going to stand out when readers are browsing.

There also seems to be a big difference in getting over that double-digit number for reviews. A book with nine or fewer reviews looks like few people have read it. Increase the reviews by just one more to 10 and you see a significant increase in sales.

A focus of your book launch is going to be to get at least ten reviews in the first few days so that random visitors to your Amazon page will get that social proof they need to buy the book. Since the people you ask reviews from are more likely to leave five-star reviews, it's also a good way to build your average star-rating up so you can withstand a few bad reviews when they come in.

Getting Ready for Your Book Launch

Your book launch doesn't just come together a few days before you publish. Getting ready for your launch will take weeks, at minimum, and must be managed if you're going to have a successful launch.

First is planning your launch date. Don't plan on launching your book over a long holiday weekend. You want people to be at their computers, which means during a weekday. Yeah, I know that many people use their phones or tablets to buy books even when they aren't at work, but traffic numbers don't lie. Amazon gets more traffic Monday through Thursday than Friday through Sunday.

Besides not being at their computer, people have better things to do on the weekend than browse Amazon for books.

The exception to this would be Black Friday and Cyber Monday. I've seen authors successfully launch during this time but it's a risky strategy. Your launch team and contacts will have more on their mind than helping support your book.

I would recommend launching on Monday or Tuesday.

Next in your pre-launch planning is lining up sales and reviews.

- Don't think that a simple Facebook post is going to be enough. People have to be asked personally through an email or message. Even after that, you'll still have to remind people on launch day and to leave a review.
- Launch for $0.99 and ask people if they will buy your book during one of the first five days of launch. At that price, it's not about the money but about getting on Amazon's paid ranking chart.
- Ask people to buy the book, wait at least a day or two and then leave a review. You can help them a little by writing out a couple of ideas for what to say in the review but don't write the same thing for everyone.

Your first step in getting book sales and reviews is to contact all the people you know through social media. You can post a message saying you are looking for people to buy the book and leave a review, but you also need to individually message each person.

Don't be shy. It takes less than a minute for someone to buy your book and less than a couple of minutes to leave a review. Let people know how much their support means to you and that you appreciate their time.

They don't have to do anything right now. Once the launch starts, you'll be contacting everyone again with a link click through and buy the book.

You also want to reach out to bloggers in the topic.

- Make a list of all the blogs in your book's topic by doing a few Google searches. 'Best [topic] Blogs' is a good start because you'll get lists of blogs in that niche.
- Go to each blog and copy down the blogger's name and email.
- Start following the blogger in social media a few months before your book launch. Comment on their posts, share and like on Facebook and retweet their Twitter feed.
- At least a month before the book launch, reach out to each blogger by email. Tell them about your launch and ask if you can write a guest post. Your guest post should be around a related topic to your book, giving readers a real solution and not just being a commercial for your book. You can add a brief paragraph on the book and how the information in it has transformed your life, along with a link to the Amazon page.
- Even if you can't get a guest post, ask each blogger if they will share your launch-day post on Facebook and retweet on Twitter.

If you have a blog (and you should because we've already talked about strategically planning your book on the blog) then you will want to start collecting emails of people interested in the book.

- Get a 300x250 and a 728x90 banner designed on Fiverr to promote your upcoming book. You can put these banners in your sidebar and on pages, promoting the special discounted price and great information in the book.
- Create a landing page or a post that talks about the book and has an email sign-up form for people interested in getting the book on the launch day. You'll link the banner ads to this page and can also link it in your posts.
- Start collecting these emails a month ahead of the launch and you'll have dozens of people waiting anxiously for your book.

There are also third-party promotion services you might want to check out. These are websites with lists of avid readers and daily traffic that can help boost your book. Not all of them are worth paying for and some require 10+ reviews on a book before they'll accept your request.

I've copied down the 14 best book promotion services I've found through my own books. Most of these will work for non-fiction books while a few are geared more towards fiction novels. The top rows have produced the best results in my experience.

Kindle Book Promotion Sites

BookBub	Buck Books	Books Butterfly
Many Books	Ereader News Today	Kindle Nation Daily
Awesome Gang	Author Marketing Club	The Kindle Book Review
Kindle Book Promos	Bargain eBook Hunter	Just Kindle Books
Book Deal Hunter	The Wall of Books	

You don't have to spend hundreds of dollars promoting your book. Try the first five or six in the list; especially BookBub, Buck Books and Books Butterfly. You'll need your Amazon page URL so this is something you'll need to set up after your book has launched but you'll want to plan for it in the pre-launch.

These book promotion services aren't necessarily to get that first push of sales but to keep generating sales after your personal network has come through. If you can schedule sales and reviews from your personal network through the first week, then get sales through promotion services in the second week of launch, you'll build much more stability in your rankings.

A few days before your launch, start getting your email subscribers and other people excited about the launch with emails and social media posts. These can be simple posts or emails with a quote from the book or an interesting statistic, how the book has transformed someone's life or a pre-publication review.

How to Do a Book Launch for Amazon Self-Publishing

The strategy for Amazon launches used to be to start as a free book and then slowly increase the price. You could get thousands of downloads which turned into a dozen reviews and helped ranking once the price was higher.

Then Amazon changed how it ranks books. It now has two separate rankings, one for free books and one for paid books. You can rank #1 as a free book but once you raise the price, it counts for nothing. All those free downloads no longer help your book ranking in the paid categories.

There are a lot of people that still recommend launching for free, mostly because they read old blog posts with the old strategy. It's really just a waste of your launch efforts.

The new strategy is to start at $0.99 for your book launch. This will put you on the paid-ranking scale immediately and you won't lose your momentum as you increase the price.

When you do finally get to your launch, I know it seems like forever, you want to do a soft launch for a few days to get your reviews.

A soft launch is where you publish your book but don't promote it out to the public yet. Instead, you reach out to your personal network to let them know the book is live. Through the soft launch, you are hoping to get those initial sales and reviews that will act as social proof when you promote the book out publicly.

1. It will take Amazon up to 24 hours but usually less than 12 hours to make your book live on the site after you click publish. You might consider doing this on Thursday or Friday, so you can start the soft launch on Saturday.
2. Email and message all your friends and family that agreed to buy the book. Give them a link to the page and ask them to buy the book over the weekend. Ask them to wait a day or two and then go back and leave a review.
3. Email and message your list again on Monday to ask them to leave a review. Let them know that it's important before you can start your official launch and

send them a link for the page again. Make sure you give them step-by-step instructions on how to leave a review.

Once you've got your 10+ reviews, you can start your official launch out to the general public.

- Email your subscribers to let them know the book is launched. You might consider offering a special handout or bonus chapter to anyone that buys within the first few days. You won't get contact info of people buying the book on Amazon so ask everyone to email you after purchasing for their bonus material.
- Email your blogger list to let them know the book is launched and thank them for their help so far. Copy a simple Tweet and a Facebook post they can use to spread the word.
- Retweet, Like and Comment on any Facebook posts or tweets mentioning your book to show your appreciation and spread the word.
- Send two tweets a day over the first five days of your public launch using interesting quotes, memes and info from the book
- Post once a day to Facebook about the launch, brag about #1 rankings achieved and include a countdown to the end of the launch to create some urgency

Search Twitter and Facebook for "Kindle Books" to find groups and handles that promote discounted books. Many of these will be targeted to free Kindle books but you can also promote your $0.99 launch.

A simple tweet like "[Title] is just $0.99 today for the special launch price. Get it now or miss out." and include the link to your page. You can try adding in a quote or short review in Facebook posts. Post in as many groups as you can over a three-day period and you'll keep your sales going strong even as the rest of your launch efforts start fading.

I spend $200 a month on ads through Amazon Marketing Services for all ten of my books. From these ads, I produce about $700 in sales which is enough when combined with sales from the blogs to keep the books ranked within the first 10 or 20 in their categories.

I'll share my strategy for using AMS ads in the next article on marketing your self-published book, but you'll want to start your ads during that first week of launch. As long as you get those 10+ reviews, you'll have enough social proof to use ads effectively.

Increase your book's price to $2.99 on the tenth day or after you've had time to get a few book promotions done at $0.99 from third-party websites. You should start seeing some consistent ranking by now on prior sales. After a few more days, increase the price to $3.99 or to the final price.

Launching a book on Amazon is a much longer process than most authors realize but it's critical to building stable rankings. If you don't spread consistent sales over at least a week or two, you run the risk of losing your rankings faster. Keeping a strong ranking in at least one category is how you get consistent sales every month and the only way to do that is to jumpstart your book with a strong launch.

Book Marketing Strategies for Passive Income

Creating a book marketing strategy will make your self-publishing almost completely passive income

This article on marketing your self-published book is by far the longest in the series of making money with books, and for good reason.

A good book launch will get you ranked on Amazon but you need consistent monthly sales to maintain those rankings. A good marketing plan will get you the handful of sales you need to keep the Amazon ranking system working for you, and send you lots of sales from readers browsing and searching the platform.

I use the three book marketing strategies below to generate 190 sales a month from Amazon Marketing Services and another 60 from my own and other websites. That 250 sales across ten books is enough to get me an average of 670 total copies sold each month.

I sell over 400 copies of my books because that small amount of marketing helps me stay ranked within each book's categories.

Best of all, the three ways to market your books are almost completely passive. Once you set each up, they'll consistently make book sales without any extra effort. It makes self-publishing one of the most passive income streams I've ever seen.

The Three-Legged Strategy for Marketing Your Self-Published Book

Your singular focus in marketing your book is to sell enough that it ranks well within its categories. That doesn't mean selling dozens of books a day. If you can sell a few dozen copies of your books each month through your own marketing, that's going to be enough to rank well in most categories.

When you rank within the top 10 in a category, people are going to see your book while browsing or searching and you'll have the opportunity to sell hundreds more through Amazon.

That's good news for us regular authors. If making sales were all on us, it would be tough driving the kind of traffic you need to make a living as a self-published author. Fortunately, Amazon gets hundreds of millions of visitors a month and wants them to buy your book.

Still, even driving a few dozen sales a month from your own blog might be tough for most bloggers. That's why you need a three-pronged strategy for getting those sales you need to help Amazon rank your book.

We'll cover each of these book marketing strategies in depth:

- Marketing on your own blog through 'best books lists' and links in related posts
- Marketing on other blogs through guest posts, podcast interviews and book lists
- Marketing through AMS for sponsored products and product display ads

The best part is that all three of these marketing strategies is almost completely passive once you set it up. Each will drive enough incremental sales to keep your book ranked in its categories and get Amazon to do the rest!

How to Market Your Self-Published Book on a Blog

Marketing your book on your own blog is the easiest and first step you should take.

Each year, create a 'Best [Topic] Books to Read' list with five to 15 books in a topic related to your niche. Get your Amazon affiliate link for each book when your linking to it in the post. Of course, your book should be one of those recommended.

These are super-easy to rank and always make me a few bucks a month from Amazon every month as well as lead to a sale or two of my own books.

If you followed my self-publishing blogger strategy then you've got five to ten posts that were turned into chapters in your book. By the time your book is published, these should be getting some Google search traffic each month. Go back in and update them with a couple of paragraphs in the intro, teasing your book and including a link.

These are easy marketing targets because the people coming from Google search are laser-focused on the topic.

You can also go back through other related posts on your blog and add a couple of paragraphs about your book. Make the description as related as possible to each post to appeal more directly to readers coming from Google search to that article. Include a text link plus a clickable image of your book.

Always remember to use your Amazon affiliate code when linking to a book on your blog. You'll get a commission on the sale plus your regular 70% for the book sale.

Selling Your Amazon Book through Other Blogs

Marketing your book through other blogs takes a little more work but will drive those extra sales you need each month.

Guest posts are a good way to get a link back to your blog for SEO plus a link to your Amazon book page. Remember the golden rule in guest posting, what's in it for the other blog's readers?

When reaching out to other bloggers for a guest post, be sure to pitch three topics that are related to their blog and to your book. Make the post about the reader, a problem they need to solve or an interesting story from which they can learn. Briefly and without being too salesy, talk about your book and how it relates to the post.

Link to your Amazon page but let the blogger know they are free to change it to their Amazon affiliate link so they will earn a commission on sales.

Podcast interviews are another great way to market your book, especially if it's a video podcast because people will be able to see your book.

As with any kind of blogger outreach marketing, you have to develop a relationship with the other bloggers first. This means following them on social media, retweeting and sharing their content, and trying to build that connection.

Put together a list of 25 - 50 podcasters within your topic. Browse through their shows and make sure they include guests. You're not aiming for Dave Ramsey here, look for podcasters that are more likely to connect but that still have decent traffic per month.

Many podcasters will provide their listener numbers in an advertising page on their blog so this can give you an idea of their reach. The sweet spot seems to be between 1,000 to 5,000 downloads per day for finding approachable podcasters. You might also target the New & Noteworthy list for easy interview targets.

Once you've spent a little time developing a relationship with each podcaster, reach out by email and offer them a free copy of your book. Tell them you respect their opinion and would love their feedback on your work.

If they like the book, it's almost a slam dunk that they'll ask you to be on the show to talk about it.

Finally, you can also reach out for inclusion in book lists on other blogs. Do a Google search for 'Best [Topic] Books to Read' and copy down the URLs of the first 50 results. Go to each website to find contact information and email the blogger. Offer a unique paragraph describing your book that they can just copy/paste into their list along with their Amazon affiliate link.

Marketing Your Book with Amazon Ads

Marketing your book on Amazon Marketing Services is easily the most effective of the three strategies but also costs the most money. You'll get a great return for your money though and will sell enough copies to keep your book ranked.

The screenshot shows just a few of the ads I have running for my books. The ACoS column is Amazon's estimate for Average Cost of Sales which is the amount you've spent on ads divided by the sales related to those ads.

You can see that these ads are costing from about 3% to 20% of sales. Put another way, I'm making between 33- and five-times the amount I spend on ads through Amazon.

Unfortunately, you can't just throw more money at AMS. We'll get to why that is later but first, let's get to starting your own AMS ads for your book.

There are two ads you can place for your book on AMS, sponsored products and product display. Both run on a pay-per-click basis meaning you only pay for advertising when someone clicks on your ad.

- Sponsored Product ads appear after the book description as 'Sponsored products related to this item' and at the bottom of search results. If you search for something on Amazon, you'll see "Sponsored" at the top of these ads.
- Product Display ads show up on the right side of Amazon book pages.

I'll cover how to set up both types of advertising for your book but, to be honest, I see 99% of my sales from sponsored product ads. Product displays seem to work better for other types of products rather than books. They can help move the needle a little on your books but sponsored product ads work much better.

The Basics of Amazon Book Marketing

The basics of Amazon book marketing are easy. You pick a type of ad and a book you want to promote. Then you pick keywords you want to target for your ad. When someone uses one of those keywords in a search or lands on a page of a related book, your book will show as a sponsored ad.

You tell Amazon the maximum amount you want to spend a day on ads and how much you're willing to spend for each time someone clicks on a keyword.

Of course, you're not the only one bidding on keywords so Amazon uses a bidding system to determine where you show up in the sponsored results. We'll get into this in more detail in the next section.

If someone clicks on your ad then you are charged a cost-per-click depending on Amazon's bidding system and the amount you tell Amazon you are willing to pay per click. The amount you pay is very rarely as much as you bid so don't worry about seeing runaway costs on ads.

Amazon Marketing Services shows a complete picture of your ads, at the campaign and at the keyword level. At the campaign-level, you'll see the following stats for each ad.

- **Campaign Name** - Be descriptive of your campaigns so you can tell them apart. You'll have several campaigns for each book so it's best to distinguish them so you can learn which strategies are working.
- **Start and End Date** - Your campaign will have a start date but I usually just let sponsored product ads run indefinitely. Product display ads will have an end date.
- **Budget** is the max amount you are willing to spend per day but I've never seen a campaign hit this max.
- **Impressions** is the number of times your ad is shown while **clicks** is the number of times someone clicks on your ad.
- **aCPC** is the average cost-per-click you've paid when someone clicks on your ad.
- **Spend** is the total amount you've spent on this campaign.
- **Est Total Sales** is the estimate for sales across all formats of your book including Kindle, paperback and audio. Note that this is total sales and not commission so this isn't the amount you've received. You actually make about 70% on Kindle, 40% on paperback and audio sales.
- **ACoS** is the spend amount divided by the estimated total sales and is a measure of your advertising profitability. Any number below 100% is profitable, meaning you are spending less than the sales you're

making from the ad. Since AMS tracks total sales and not your actual commissions, this measure isn't exact. To be more accurate, I would say an ACoS below 60% is a better measure of a profitable ad.

Unlike other advertising platforms like Google Adwords where you want to pick only highly-relevant keywords, the secret to Amazon marketing is to use as many keywords as possible. You can have up to 1,000 keywords in each campaign and you'll run several campaigns for each book.

One of my best book campaigns has gotten 1.34 million impressions and made $2,219 in total sales, for a 22% ACoS. That's only about 652 sales or a rate of 0.049% on impressions. That's actually a good rate of sales so you see how you need to target thousands of keywords and get millions of impressions to sell as many books as possible.

Starting a Sponsored Product Ad for Your Book

After creating your Amazon Marketing Services account, you'll click on 'New Campaign' to start an ad. Then choose a sponsored product or product display ad.

You'll then select which book you want to advertise and will start creating your ad details.

- Campaign Name - Be descriptive here on the types of keywords or strategy you want to use. That way you'll be able to see which strategies or keyword ideas are working best and can use them on other books.
- Average Daily Budget - I start with $15 a day but have never seen a campaign use the full amount. You'll only be paying about $0.10 per click and most campaigns will get less than a few clicks a day.
- Duration - I always just let these run continuously to make my book marketing passive.

- Select 'Manual Targeting' to pick your keywords for the book. You can also run one campaign on 'Automatic Targeting' to see how it does.
- Add keywords you'd like to target for the ad. I usually run one campaign that just targets the Amazon suggested keywords and then several campaigns targeting keywords I select. Start with a bid of $0.25 for all keywords.

Just like your daily budget, you will rarely (if ever) spend as much on a click as your bid. I average between $0.08 to $0.27 a click on dozens of campaigns and thousands of keywords even though I'm bidding $0.40 for many and as high as $1.00 per click for some.

The reason you want to set your daily budget and keyword bid high is because it works into Amazon's bidding system. Amazon's bidding system factors in your budget, keyword bid and how relevant the book is to the keyword to estimate the potential for a sale.

Remember, Amazon makes money off sales as well as the marketing costs. It wants to show books that will maximize its profit in both so it is going to rank your ad higher if you bid higher.

Amazon only charges you when someone clicks on an ad and the cost-per-click is only as high as the next lower bid for that keyword. That's why, while you might bid $0.25 for a keyword, you'll only pay maybe $0.09 when someone clicks on your ad.

The final piece of your ad is filling in the text you want to appear. This is very important for two reasons.

- Obviously, you want to make your ad attractive and enticing to get people to your book description so you can make the sale.

- You also want to screen readers by making your text as descriptive as possible. You only want people clicking on your ad that are going to be interested in your book's topic.

Make sure to include emotional triggers in your ad and the transformational idea readers are looking for in the topic. Create a sense of urgency with time-related words like today, now or fast.

After you've perfected your text, click 'Launch Campaign' and your ad will be reviewed for publication. Most ads are approved and start running within a day. In my experience, the biggest problem with ad denials is in the text and Amazon will tell you why it denies an ad.

Finding Keywords for Marketing Your Book

Finding keywords for marketing your book is where you'll spend most of your time when creating ads.

You need at least a few hundred keywords for each campaign and should run at least four or five campaigns for each book. You won't necessarily keep all these keywords or campaigns running forever but you want to start out testing as large a list as possible.

1) If you have blog articles related to the topic or chapters you published, you can use Google Search Console to download a list of search terms for which the articles are ranking. Go to your blog on Search Console, click 'Search Analytics' and then toggle 'Pages' to find the article and download all the queries into a list.

2) Don't just stop at your blog articles. Use Ahrefs to find the search keywords for articles on other websites related to your book's topic.

- Search Google for a few of your most relevant keywords and copy the URL address for the top five results.
- Go to Ahrefs and paste each URL into the Site Explorer search.
- Click on 'Organic Keywords' and filter for 0-20 in Position, export the results in a list.

3) Create another keyword list using titles of books from the Amazon Best Sellers list in your categories. Click through to each sub-category and copy the titles of the top 30 books as well as the most popular authors' names. People are going to be directly searching for these books so you might as well ride along on their popularity.

4) You can also use Google Adwords to find keyword suggestions. Start an Adwords campaign on an article that is highly-related to your book topic. This doesn't have to be an article of yours, any that is relevant to your book.

You'll copy the URL of the article into the campaign and Google will give you keyword suggestions for your Adwords campaign. You don't actually have to start the campaign, just copy these keywords into a list for your Amazon campaigns.

5) Click through to each of the highest ranked books in your categories and copy the titles of the 'Customers also bought' books and the sponsored books. Some of these will be repeats of the titles you copied from your best-seller list so remove any duplicates.

6) You'll also brainstorm a list of your most relevant keywords. Type these words into Amazon and Google to get more suggestions from the drop-down search. Searching for your

keywords on Google will also give you a few more ideas from the 'People also ask' section and the 'People also searched for' section at the bottom of the page.

7) Use a keyword density checker online on your book's text to find the phrases most often used in your book. These are going to be highly-relevant keywords since you're using them naturally in the text.

These seven steps should give you thousands of keyword ideas for your book campaigns. You'll want to create multiple campaigns so you can keep keyword strategies separate and see which perform best.

Starting a Product Display Ad for Your Book

Starting a product display ad is very similar to the sponsored product ad process for your book. Click on 'New Campaign', select Product Display and which book you'd like to advertise.

You can target your ad by product, showing your book to people looking at similar books, or by interest where you book will be shown on Kindle E-readers and within categories on Amazon. Run a campaign in each of these to see how each does. You can always stop an unprofitable campaign and you really want to test all your options.

Within the 'by product' option, you can target specific books or related categories. Targeting specific products, you'll be able to enter keywords and product names and Amazon will generate a list of potential products on which to show your ad.

This is where you want to get creative with your targeting.

- Target other books that appear when you put in your most relevant keywords
- Target books in related categories and topics
- Target popular authors or bloggers in your topic

- Target new and popular books that might be heavily promoted right now

Within the 'by interest' option, you'll select categories on which to advertise your book. You don't necessarily need to select only the categories most related to your book's topic. Think about your own reading habits, you don't just read books within one topic.

You'll then place a bid for your cost-per-click and the campaign budget. Notice this isn't a daily budget but one for your entire campaign. The minimum here is $100 and a good place to start with your campaigns.

You will also need a start and end date for product display ads. The default is usually two months and I usually leave it as that. I also usually choose to 'Run campaign as quickly as possible' in the Pacing option rather than 'Spread campaign evenly over its duration'. This will promote your book as heavily as possible, which is what you want to really boost ranking.

Finally, you'll customize your ad text just like you did with sponsored product ads. In product display ads, you'll also get the chance to add a headline. Search for some of your keywords on Google and note the most interesting titles in the results for potential headlines.

Amazon will show you how your ad will look on Kindle as well as the three other size of ads for Product Display and where they will appear. If you like how your ad looks, click to submit your campaign.

Managing your Amazon Book Marketing Ads

It will take a few days for impressions of your ads to start showing in your campaign and maybe weeks to start really seeing any clicks and sales. The click-through and conversion rate on Amazon ads is horrendously low. Even on good ads, only about 0.2% of your impressions will get clicked and only 10% to 20% of those clicks will lead to a sale.

That's ok though because you'll be getting millions of impressions across all your campaigns and will make enough sales to keep your book ranked in its categories. Keeping your category rankings is all that matters because that means you'll make lots of sales from people browsing and searching on Amazon.

After about a month, you can go into a campaign to fine-tune your bidding and keywords.

Click on the campaign name in Amazon Marketing Services and you'll be taken to your keywords and general campaign settings.

You'll be able to see each keyword and all its detail for your campaign. I've deleted the actual keywords from the screenshot here. You can see that I've increased my bid a lot for these profitable keywords. Test increasing your CPC bid in increments of $0.10 until the ACoS reaches around 40% to get the most impressions and sales possible.

You can also decrease or delete keywords that are not profitable, i.e. an ACoS of 80% or higher. I would usually keep a keyword or campaign running even if the ACoS is as high as 100%. You may be losing a little bit on the ad but the sales you get here will mean a higher ranking and more organic sales on your book.

Final Tips and Tricks to Successful Marketing for Your Self-Published Book

Most of your sales through marketing will happen through your Amazon Marketing ads. That means testing a massive list of keywords in multiple campaigns per book to see what works.

It's not unusual for me to develop a dozen ad campaigns for a book, each with hundreds of keywords.

Let your campaigns run for a couple of months and then revise them once a month for the next three months. Increase your bid on highly-profitable keywords and decrease or delete highly-unprofitable keywords.

The great thing about pay-per-click campaigns is that you only pay when someone clicks on your ad. If your cover image, title and description tell potential readers exactly what they can expect then they're only likely to click on your ad if they are interested in buying. That means you can advertise on a huge range of keywords, even in seemingly unrelated books and topics, and still get a good average cost-per-sale.

Don't forget that you also want to have all three formats of your book available while you're running ads. At the minimum, you should have a Kindle and paperback version available, but I would create an audio version as well. If you're going to pay when someone clicks through to your book's page, you want to give them every opportunity possible to buy.

Marketing your book is one of the biggest factors in making consistent sales every month. You don't have to be an expert marketer. You just need to drive a few sales through marketing to keep Amazon's ranking program working for you. A good book marketing program is almost completely automated and will mean passive income self-publishing for all your books.

10 Self-Publishing Mistakes Every New Author Makes

Avoid these biggest self-publishing mistakes and you'll be ready to make money on your first book

There are nearly two million books available on Amazon and I bet twice that number of books started but never finished. Even among the self-published books finished and for sale on the world's largest ecommerce platform, the majority make less than $50 a month.

The tragedy in this is that self-publishing is EASY!

It doesn't take a rocket scientist to write a book and make money on Amazon. The problem is the misconceptions and the self-publishing mistakes new authors make that dooms their book from day one.

Besides the ten books I've self-published, I've consulted and helped more than a hundred authors get started. Within that number, ten mistakes have emerged as almost universal and the biggest challenges you'll face writing your book.

Self-Publishing Mistakes Getting Started

The first mistakes most new authors keep them from getting started or keeping the momentum to get their book done. As bad as some of the other mistakes are, these are the worst because they keep you from finishing and keep you from learning from your mistakes.

1) One of the simplest things you can do to help finish your book is to set a detailed schedule and deadline. The problem most authors face is they don't understand the entire process

that goes into developing, writing and publishing a book. Fair enough but once you know the process, you can create a schedule that hits each point.

Reading through the book, list out each step and make notes under each for what goes into it. Starting from today's date, add a deadline date for the first step then days to complete that step and a deadline. You might have to adjust some of the dates a little as you go and understand better how much time it takes to complete but this kind of strict scheduling is going to help you stay on track.

Steps in the Book Publishing Process

- Deciding your book idea and researching other books on Amazon
- Outlining your book from transformation back through each step
- Outlining each chapter idea
- Writing each chapter separately
- Combining your chapters, reading through for flow and adding content to fill in the gaps
- Formatting for self-publishing
- Creating a book cover
- Creating a marketing plan and launch strategy
- Launching your book
- Marketing strategies to keep your book ranked

2) One thing that almost nobody does but will give you the support and motivation you need is to share your self-publishing goals with friends. Tell them about your deadline and ask them about their goals. Then keep each other accountable by asking about progress every couple of weeks.

Better yet, connect with a few other self-publishers for a weekly mastermind group. This is just a group of three to five people that meet online every week or two. You exchange ideas, talk about your progress and ask questions to overcome challenges. It's a great way to get the support and answers you need to stay on track and be successful.

3) Part of that scheduling mistake new authors make is not outlining your chapters and breaking the work into chunks. Just sitting down to the computer to write your book is a fast route to writer's block. Even the experienced authors don't set out that way.

Taking each chapter one at a time not only makes for a great marketing strategy through your blog, it'll also make each chapter easier to write. Instead of struggling with the big book idea, you'll be focused on the smaller chapter idea and know exactly what you need to write about.

4) Beating this next mistake is a bummer for most new authors...but here it is. You have to treat your self-publishing like a job. Set yourself goals and responsibilities for every week. Set aside time to write every day and don't make excuses.

You see, a lot of self-publishers approach it as something they'd like to do. They've always wanted to write a book and it would be nice to make a little extra money. Why not give it a try?

I'm all for enjoying your side hustle and the last thing you want is another 'job' but you have to set that must-finish mentality with your book. You need to make it a commitment or your book will end up in the bottomless pile of unfinished projects.

New Author Mistakes that Ruin Your Book

It might surprise you that only two of the ten mistakes is around creating a quality book. That's not to say that you can produce a crap book and make sales.

The fact is that most people spend plenty of time researching their book. It starts from an area of experience and really drives a transformation in the readers. The reality is that most books, if they ever get written are good reads. It's the parts of the process that authors don't fully understand like marketing and being a professional author that trips people up.

There are two mistakes on the content-side that you will need to avoid though.

5) Many non-fiction authors fall into the trap of just writing out their book in a straight-forward, how-to style. The work backwards from the transformation and check every box in the steps someone needs to take to get there.

And the book ends up being SOOOO boring!

Bring your book to life with personal stories, anecdotes and examples. This not only shows readers how the ideas are applied in real life but gives them something to relate to and inspire their transformation. It's best if these stories come out naturally as you're writing but go back through after writing to make sure you have at least an example or two in each chapter.

6) Another big mistake I see a lot of new self-publishing authors make is trying to edit their own book. I know what you're thinking. Editing can be a big expense, easily the biggest. You're not ready to put down a few hundred dollars or more on something you don't will even make any money.

The problem is, you're just too close to the material. You've spent the last 12 weeks writing this book and countless hours. You know what you wrote and you know the process from start to finish. What happens when you sit down to edit, you just want to get it done and move on to publish.

The result, you'll end up skipping over sections. You'll zone out and not really check the reading. You'll also fall into all the assumptions someone makes when they already know the material.

You need a fresh set of eyes on your book for editing, preferably someone that doesn't know much about the subject of the book.

You don't need to spend a lot on editing but you will need to spend something. Start on Craigslist or on the job board at the local community college. You're not looking for an English major, just someone that can tell you where the story doesn't flow and parts they don't understand. In self-publishing, it's the story and readability much more than the grammar.

Self-Publishing Mistakes to Sell More Books

The dirty little secret of self-publishing is that it's not your book that sells, it's your marketing.

Really this is the tragic truth in any business. It sucks that you can't just create a great product. You still won't make a dime unless you put together a great marketing strategy to get that product in front of the right people, at the right time.

Since most new authors don't realize this, there are a lot of mistakes made.

7) The first mistake here is just not using a blog or some other distribution resource strategically. You're already writing content and making notes from your research, it takes almost no time to turn that time into a blog or YouTube channel.

Posting your book chapters on a blog or turning them into videos will help to keep you on schedule and get your book finished. More than that however, a blog will be one of your best marketing resources. Without a blog or some other channel, you're stuck trying to advertise your book for the sales you need to keep your book ranked.

It costs very little to start a blog, less than $3 a month with this special deal from Bluehost. Your blog will do most of the work in your marketing plan and can even become an asset by itself, bringing in sponsorships and affiliate commissions.

8) Another mistake I see even the experienced authors make is not being more direct with friends and family. The mistake goes like this, everything is ready to launch the book and the author puts out a post on Facebook. The post asks everyone to help out by sharing the book launch, buying a copy at the discounted price and leaving a review.

Then nothing happens!

Not only is the book launch a total failure but the author comes out hurt and rejected thinking even their friends and family don't support them.

Your friends and family DO want to support you, but it takes more than just a generic social media post to get them to do anything. Think about it. How many Facebook and Twitter posts do you see each day? How many do you remember three seconds after seeing them and how many do you even take the time to 'like' or share?

We have 'social media blindness' and even the pleas for help rarely break it.

Instead, you need to personally reach out through a direct message or even a phone call to people for your launch. Even an email might not be enough to get a real commitment.

- Send out a direct message to each social media contact asking if they'll help out by buying a copy during the launch day and leaving a review.
- Reach out by phone to the people that don't reply to your direct message.
- Send a direct message the first day of the launch asking again for their support.
- Send a reminder message on the third day of your launch with the urgency that the launch is almost over.

Remember, you need at least 10 reviews during your launch and as many sales as you can get. Remind people that it's not really about the money. You'll be launching at $0.99 so nobody is paying or making a lot of money, it's just about the support and getting that momentum.

9) Part of making as much money as possible on your self-published book is offering it to as many people as possible. It always surprises me how many people still buy paperback books, despite the fact the price is about twice that of an ebook, but some people are just physical book people.

Fortunately, it takes almost no effort to format your ebook for a print copy. You can do it from the same file you upload to Amazon Kindle with just a few changes. Creating a print-on-demand format for your book will double your sales and help keep both formats ranked.

It takes more work but I would also recommend creating an audio format for sale on Audible. This might be more expensive for fiction authors since you'll need to hire actors for the characters but non-fiction writers can read their own book. Besides being listed on audiobook site Audible, you'll also have your audiobook listing on the main Amazon page. This gives your book maximum reach for any type of customer.

10) The final mistake most new authors make is quitting after writing one book. I know you're hoping that this first book hits and you make thousands a month...but sometimes it just doesn't work like that.

Of the ten books I've published, I make as much as $500 a month on a couple but there are a few than make $100 or less some months. Sometimes a book just isn't as popular as you thought it would be.

Create a library of at least a few books though and your monthly sales will average out. You'll make around two or three hundred per book each month and will have the start of a very nice passive income stream.

Don't get discouraged if a book isn't the lottery ticket you thought it would be. Move on to the next book, try to understand why the last one didn't hit and build your online income!

Self-publishing a book isn't difficult. Thousands of people start on their book idea every month only to give up or never finish. It's these ten self-publishing mistakes that account for the vast majority of that failure. Learn how to avoid these mistakes and you'll be ready to create the book you always wanted to write.

Resources to Write and Market Your Book

This list of resources will get you started on some of the tools and services I use to make self-publishing as easy as possible. You don't need all of them but learn to use them right and you'll be able to publish and sell more books than you ever imagined possible!

Amazon Resources for Self-Publishing

Amazon Author Central – Create an author page, track your rankings and monitor customer reviews. Author Central is a must-know site apart from your main KDP dashboard.

Amazon Marketing Services – Where you'll set up your ad campaigns for each book, pick keywords and set a budget. With a small marketing campaign for each book, you'll keep it ranked and making organic sales for hundreds a month.

Audible ACX – is the audio format publisher owned by Amazon and how you'll offer your book as an audiobook.

Marketing Tools for Self-Publishing

Bluehost – A blog isn't a must for self-publishing authors but it will help more than you can imagine and can become its own money-making asset. I make thousands on my blogs each month and they provide easy [FREE] marketing for the books. Launching a blog means you'll need to register a domain and get webhosting, both available through Bluehost.

ConvertKit – I used three other email marketing tools and none of them had the features I needed, until ConvertKit. The site makes it easy to get email subscribers from your blog, send out automated email sequences and sell more books. Easily the best marketing tool for the money.

Teachable – Video courses are the next level for self-publishing authors and Teachable is my go-to resource. The site is a one-stop for creating, marketing and delivering a video course to make money. You can even sign up other people to sell your course for you as affiliates, all on the Teachable platform.

Finding Freelancers to Help with Your Books

Upwork – is where I go to find most freelancers, especially if I already have a detailed idea of how I want the project to develop. The freelancer marketplace has its share of bad servicers but spend the time to interview and test for the right one and you'll build your team in no time.

Fiverr – I generally use Fiverr when I need help developing an idea. Since the projects are cheaper than hiring a freelancer on Upwork, I can buy a few 'gigs' to get ideas and test out different designs before going all-in on one. Works great for getting cover ideas and other design elements.

Thank You for Taking Me on Your Journey

Just one last note to say, Thank You, for starting your journey with me. I'm excited about what lies ahead and I know it's going to change your life.

There is no other income source I've enjoyed more than self-publishing and no other has created the same level of passive income. The internet revolution has given us all the power to reach millions of people, transform lives and create the financial freedom we deserve.

Whether you're writing to become financially independent, help or entertain others, you'll be able to do it all with self-publishing.

I want to continue to be a part of your journey. Know that I'm always available to answer questions or just be a source for motivation when you need it. Reach out by email or through comments on the videos at Let's Talk Money on YouTube.

To your success,

Joseph Hogue

Joseph Hogue, CFA

Printed in Great
Britain
by Amazon